Rocks and
Minerals

Adrian Jones

Collins

An Imprint of HarperCollins*Publishers*

ISBN-10: 0-00-717794-1
ISBN-13: 978-0-00-717794-3

ISBN-10: 0-06-084983-5 (in the United States)
ISBN-13: 978-0-06-084983-2
FIRST U.S. EDITION Published in 2006

HarperCollins books may be purchased for educational, business, or sales promotional use. For information in the United States, please write to: Special Markets Department, HarperCollins Publishers, 10 East 53rd Street, New York, NY 10022.

The name of the "Smithsonian," "Smithsonian Institution," and the sunburst logo are registered trademarks of the Smithsonian Institution.

Text © Adrian Jones 2000
Adrian Jones (PhD Durham) has worked in the Department of Earth Sciences, University College London since 1990. He has been collaborating with the Natural History Museum on rare earth minerals and carbonatites since his return to the UK from the California Institute of Technology in the late 1980s. His Diamond Research Group focus on the detailed origins of high pressure diamond, and recent experiments have extended to impact shock effects and melting in terrestrial meteoritic materials.

Photographs © The Natural History Museum, apart from those that appear on the following pages: Adrian P. Jones 97, 107, 121, 143, 146, 162, 165–169, 171–178, 180–183, 186–190, 192, 194–200, 202–203, 205, 208, 211, 213–219, 221–226, 228, 233–239.

10 09 08 07 06
8 7 6 5 4 3 2 1

Color origination by Colourscan, Singapore
Printed and bound by Printing Express Ltd., Hong Kong

HOW TO USE THIS BOOK

This book describes and illustrates 220 of the more common minerals and rocks. Each specimen has a separate page carrying a clear color photograph of its ideal form, as found in a professional collection, such as in a museum or university. For each specimen there is an ID Fact File listing its key features, which will help you make an accurate identification. The accompanying text provides a brief description of the specimen, with points of interest, additional aids in identification, and some basic indication of how the mineral or rock is formed or where in North America, Europe, and throughout the world it is known to occur.

The different mineral and rock groups are dealt with in the following order. Individual specimens within each group appear alphabetically.

Minerals
Native elements pp.13–19
Sulfides pp.20–42
Halides pp.43–45
Oxides/hydroxides pp.46–61
Carbonates pp.62–73
Sulfates pp.74–78
Phosphates pp.79–83
Silicates pp.84–154
Boro-silicates pp.155–157
Borates pp.158
Organic pp.159–160

Rocks
Igneous pp.161–197
Metamorphic pp.198–214
Sedimentary pp.215–233
Extraterrestrial and impact pp.234–240

Rocks will normally bear a close resemblance to the photographs. Owing to their natural variability in size and form, many minerals may differ considerably from their photographs. However, all is not lost, because minerals have distinctive crystal shapes, colors, and nearly constant physical properties that can be tested. When all of their features are considered together, it is usually possible to identify most minerals when they are presented as a hand specimen. Some minerals are just very difficult to identify or to distinguish one from another, even for the experts, and definitive tests usually require laboratory chemical analysis. There are some suggestions on pp.11–12 for further resources and contacts.

Minerals represent specific concentrations of chemical elements, and many are used as the primary source of chemicals. The vast majority of minerals are harmless, and very few have sufficient concentrations of toxic elements, or some other unique hazard, to warrant caution when handling them repeatedly; avoid inhaling or tasting minerals with your tongue!

MINERALS

Minerals are naturally occurring chemical elements or compounds with a specific composition enabling them to be classified according to their chemical group (e.g. hydrous silicate) or family name (e.g. mica). For each mineral, information about the family name, chemical group, and composition is given at the top of the page. In addition, all minerals possess a set of distinctive characteristics or properties that can aid identification. The following pages describe the most important identifying features for minerals and the terms that are commonly used in the Fact File.

Nearly all minerals have unique crystalline structures and they often occur with characteristic shapes or forms. All minerals belong to one of seven **crystal systems**, which describe the internal symmetry in the arrangement of their component atoms or molecules as mirrored frequently in their external development of crystal faces. The crystal system to which each mineral belongs is indicated by a symbol in the top left-hand corner of the page, as well as named in the Fact File. Additional artwork for each mineral shows the crystal shape for ideal crystals. The illustrations shown below represent the seven principal crystal systems.

The **color** of many minerals is distinctive, whereas many

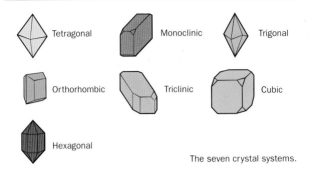

The seven crystal systems.

may also show a wide variety of colors. Use only the color of a freshly broken surface. Many sulfide and other metallic minerals often develop a surface tarnish. This differs from the true color but may also be useful for identification purposes.

The **form** in which a mineral occurs is an attempt to describe in an intuitive way its most obvious physical appearance. The main categories include whether or not individual crystal shapes are likely to be observed (crystalline), as solitary crystals or in groups (aggregates), the shapes of the crystals (equant, fibrous, radiating, and so on). Commonly, large masses may occur with no individual crystal definition (massive) or with many small crystals (granular).

Cleavage is the way some minerals split along planes of weakness related to the molecular structure and parallel to possible crystal faces. The perfection of the cleavage describes in a qualitative way how well developed it is, from imperfect (as in apatite) through good to perfect (as in mica).

Hardness is used in an approximate way to identify minerals according to Moh's scale of hardness (*see* overleaf). For example, flourite is harder than calcite and less hard than apatite. If an unknown mineral will scratch all the minerals in the scale up to 4 and is scratched by 5, its hardness is somewhere between 4 and 5. Check carefully that there is really a scratch and avoid testing on valuable crystals! Some convenient standards to use in the field include your fingernail (2.5), a penny (3), a steel penknife (5.5), a window glass (5.5), and a hardened steel file (6.5).

Relative and absolute hardness scale

Moh's hardness	Comparison mineral	Simple means of testing hardness	Absolute hardness
1	Talc	Easily scratched with fingernail	0.03
2	Gypsum	Can be scratched with fingernail	1.25
3	Calcite	Can be scratched with a penny	4.5
4	Fluorite	Easily scratched with knife	5.0
5	Apatite	Can be scratched with knife	6.5
6	Orthoclase	Can be scratched with steel file	37
7	Quartz	Scratches window glass	120
8	Topaz		175
9	Corundum		1,000
10	Diamond		140,000

Specific gravity (SG) is the relative weight of a mineral compared to the weight of an equal volume of water (and is a dimensionless equivalent to density). SG can be estimated with practice and varies significantly. For example, sulfur and halite are low (2–2.1), compared with common calcite and quartz (~2.7), while sulfides like pyrite (~5) and native metallic elements like copper (~9) and gold (~19) can be high.

Luster depends on the resorption, reflection, or refraction of light by a fresh mineral surface. Several terms are used: adamantine (brilliant) like diamond; metallic (like metal) like galena; vitreous (glassy) like quartz; also, greasy, pearly, silky, earthy, or dull. More than one luster term indicates the range shown by different forms of that mineral.

Transparency is the degree to which light passes through a mineral, and ranges from transparent like quartz, through translucent like apatite to opaque (no light passes through) like pyrite.

Other simple physical tests listed vary from mineral to mineral, but often include **fracture**, a description of the surfaces when the mineral is broken, for instance when hit with a hammer; it may be conchoidal (shell-like) like quartz, hackly, uneven, or brittle. The **streak** describes the color of the powdered mineral when rubbed against a piece of unglazed white porcelain. Many carbonates react with dilute hydrochloric acid by fizzing and releasing bubbles of gas (carbon dioxide). Additionally very few minerals are magnetic, like magnetite (which is very common), or strongly radioactive like uraninite (which is uncommon or rare). Finally for many minerals, lookalikes give a suggestion of which minerals may share similar properties or appearance to the one listed.

Where indicates within which broad classification of rocks (*see* next section) the mineral is likely to be found, and could be used in conjunction with a geological map. **Abundance** gives a rough idea of how common the mineral is in general, though of course at specific locations, like mines or quarries, this has reduced meaning; rock-forming is the most abundant where the mineral occurs in major, bulk quantities. Other terms are self-explanatory; abundant, common, uncommon, restricted, rare.

ROCKS

Rocks are solid large masses of material making up the Earth's crust. A rock may consist of just one mineral, like quartz, dolomite, or calcite. Some rocks do not have discrete minerals but are made of glasses. However, most rocks contain several minerals, or were formed from older rocks where these minerals were present. The scientific study of rocks is called petrology. The main classification of rocks is based on their fundamental origin. **Igneous** rocks solidify from molten rock, called magma, which is emplaced into and onto the crust during volcanic activity. **Sedimentary** rocks are formed at the Earth's surface by weathering of older rocks or by chemical accumulations, some of which are associated with prolific biological activity. **Metamorphic** rocks are formed by the transformation of older rocks in response to high pressures and high temperatures either during crustal mountain building or adjacent to massive cooling bodies of igneous magma. The approximate volume proportions of these three rock types throughout the Earth's crust are: igneous rocks 65%; metamorphic rocks 27%; sedimentary rocks 8%. A fourth rock category is **meteoritic** rocks, which are rare extraterrestrial rocks including very rare fragments derived from the Moon and from Mars; they share some features of all three terrestrial rock types.

Igneous Rocks

All igneous rocks are derived from magma, which forms when the Earth's interior (the upper mantle) melts; they are by far the commonest type of rocks in the Earth's crust. When this fluid magma intrudes the crust and cools very slowly, coarse crystal textures develop in coarse-grained plutonic rocks. If the magma is erupted through volcanoes onto the Earth's surface the same material is called lava; lava often cools down very quickly to form rocks with very small crystals, or fine-grained igneous rocks often containing glass. With few exceptions, igneous or magmatic rocks have compositions based on silica (SiO_2). The total silica content of an igneous rock expressed as a percentage of silica, gives one of four possible categories of chemical group for igneous rocks; acid (>66%), intermediate (52–66%), basic (44–52%), and ultrabasic (<44%). Classifications for igneous rocks rely primarily on the nature and proportions of their constituent minerals (or glass), and additionally on the relationship between their minerals, or their texture.

The igneous rocks are arranged into groups of coarse-grained, fine-grained, and volcanic rocks. The key features are listed for each igneous rock under the ID Fact File, starting with a list of **essential minerals** that should be present, and a variety of other minerals that may also be present. The **mineral proportions** are listed in terms of priority; this is considered sufficient for identifications in this book, since more scientific classifications are highly quantitative and usually require additional examination of a specially prepared thin rock slice, under a polarized-light geological microscope.

Textural features can often help in identifying a rock; the textures are described avoiding technical terms wherever possible, and can usually be discerned using a hand lens.

The **distribution** of the rock indicates the style or form of the igneous rock; coarse-grained varieties, like gabbro, form large intrusions or plutons, which can extend for miles, medium-grained igneous rocks like dolerite, form in relatively shallow sheetlike minor intrusions called sills (nearly horizontal) or dykes (nearly vertical), usually meter-scale widths. Volcanic rocks frequently contain glass and may record shattered crystals and other evidence of violent eruptions; remember steep-sided volcanoes are much more dangerous than low-shield volcanoes. The **abundance** of an igneous rock is largely subjective and should be taken only as a very rough guide.

As for minerals, lookalikes are suggested since some rocks can look similar, and this will aid identification. The text for each igneous rock provides additional information, usually with examples of European locations. These can be cross-referenced at the library, on the Internet, or through other resources.

Metamorphic Rocks

There are four main groups of metamorphic rocks, all of which have undergone change. Regional metamorphic rocks may extend for hundreds of miles, and are formed from preexisting rocks (igneous, metamorphic, or sedimentary) in response to, for example, major Earth movements, or collision of crustal tectonic plates, as associated with mountain-building. Contact metamorphic rocks form as a result of the high heat around large cooling igneous bodies and may extend for a few miles. Cataclastic rocks are mechanically crushed and powdered rocks formed by extreme deformation. Shock metamorphic rocks are produced by crater-forming impacts (*see* Extraterrestrial rocks). Chemical changes may include re-crystallization, replacement of minerals or gains or losses of chemical components during invasion by reactive fluids.

The content of entries for metamorphic rocks is broadly similar to that for igneous rocks as above except for the following.

The chemical grouping is generally more variable, reflecting wider acceptable limits for the minerals making up the named rock; **typical minerals** is less specific than "essential minerals."

The **grain size** and texture are generally more significant for identification of metamorphic rocks than proportions of minerals. An additional textural observation, **foliation**, qualitatively describes how strongly aligned mineral bands or grain size variations may be aligned causing planes of weakness across hand specimens and metamorphic rocks in outcrop.

The **conditions** refer to the general pressure temperature (P-T) conditions for formation of the rock. As examples, high grade metamorphic rocks from the lower crust, like granulite, have generally experienced the highest P-T conditions with temperatures near 3 GPa, 1,292°F, at which point the rock may begin to melt (anatexis; *see* migmatite, p.208). Contact metamorphic rocks, like hornfels, generally have minerals which attest to their high-T low-P (<1 GPa) formation. The low temperature boundary where metamorphism begins and diagenesis of sedimentary rocks ends (*see* below) is around 392–572°F. Shock metamorphism in rocks like suevite extends to tremendously high pressures (10–100 GPa).

Sedimentary Rocks

Sedimentary rocks are extremely varied; they cover about 70% of the Earth's surface. Major sedimentary layers can form slowly over very long periods of time, perhaps millions of years. Chemical classifications are more variable, and the Family indicates the general class and chemical affinity of sedimentary rock. Once transported by water, wind, or gravity, and deposited, sediments undergo diagenesis, and compaction, involving physical, chemical, and biological processes which transform loose sediments into sedimentary rock. There are four main groups: clastic or siliciclastic sediments consist of fragments of preexisting rocks transported and deposited by physical processes; biogenic sediments are largely of biological and organic origin like limestone; chemical sediments form as precipitates from solution and include evaporites and ironstones; volcaniclastic sediments usually combine siliciclastic materials with contemporaneous products of volcanic activity.

The entries for sedimentary rocks are similar in many respects to both igneous and metamorphic rocks, but with important differences. In addition to minerals, **typical components** may include older rock (lithic) fragments, and fossil debris. Their **material proportions** can vary more widely than for igneous or metamorphic rocks. Physical sediments often show signs of sorting and grain size is an important criterion for classification; with increasing grain size, fine-grained clay (<0.004 mm) grades up into silt (<0.062 mm) and then sand (<2 mm); coarse grain terminology is summarised under the entry for breccia (p.216). Textural features describe both characteristics of hand specimens, and also of the larger scale sedimentary rock exposed as an outcrop. Most sedimentary rocks show subparallel lines representing discrete accumulations known as bedding. Sorting by sedimentation often produces graded bedding with coarse grains at the base, finer grains concentrated upward. The text entry may list typical locations and also geological eras where the sedimentary rock is well represented in Europe.

Extraterrestrial Rocks

Listed under this category are true extraterrestrials, the meteorites, and also rare shock metamorphic rocks created during formation of impact craters. There are three main families of meteorites, all of which are rare; irons, stony irons, and stony meteorites, each with distinctive essential mineral content and textural features. Most meteorite specimens have a dark fusion crust at their edge where they were melted or vaporized by frictional heating during their brief passage through the Earth's atmosphere. The rarest meteorite is believed to have been blasted from the surface of Mars; it is a true Martian rock and was once thought to contain evidence of fossils implying that there has been life on Mars.

Three shock metamorphic rocks are presented to illustrate the products of large impacts on the Earth's crust. Impactite is a melt rock formed near the base of an impact crater when energy from impact is transferred as heat into the target rock. Tektite is a drop of impact melt jetted at high velocity from the impact site, which quenches to a streamlined glass in air and is deposited hundreds or thousands of miles away. Suevite is a breccia formed as a chaotic mixture of cold and hot rock particles and other rock fragments within or close to the crater itself. Some relic minerals (e.g. stishovite: *see* quartz, p.124) within suevites record evidence of the highest known shock pressures on Earth.

WHAT NEXT?

If you find you need more information about minerals and rocks, or particular locations, or would like to get in touch with others with similar interests, contact the American Federation of Mineralogical Societies (www.amfed.org). The Federation is made up of seven regional organizations. Their website gives lists of clubs, societies, schools, and organizations associated with the AFMS categorized state by state. You can also contact them by writing to the AFMS Central Office, P.O. Box 302, Glyndon, MD 21071-0302.

If you would like to see a premium collection of minerals and rocks, including fabulous gems and meteorites, the Smithsonian National Museum of Natural History (10th Street and Constitution Ave., NW, Washington, D.C. 20560) offers a world-class display. Visit the Annenberg Hooker Hall of Geology, Gems, and Minerals, where among other things, you can see the Hope Diamond. Or, you can visit the American Museum of Natural History (Central Park West at 79th Street, New York, NY 10024-5192). It contains one of the most outstanding collections of geological specimens anywhere. The museum acquired the most geologically significant rocks from regions ranging from Indonesian volcanoes to the Sahara Desert, and features displays including 168 rock specimens and 11 full-scale models of classic outcroppings from 25 countries.

The Geological Society of America, established in 1888, provides support to earth scientists at all levels. Their website (www.geosociety.org) has, among other things, a bookstore, an online journal, and information about awards and grants. You can write to them at P.O. Box 9140, Boulder, CO 80301-9140.

The homepage of the website of the Association of American State Geologists (www.stategeologists.org) shows a U.S. map. Click on any state to see the Geological Survey of that state and find links offering related geological information.

Collins publishes the following recommended guides:
Collins Photoguide Rocks, Minerals and Gemstones by W. Schumann, HarperCollins*Publishers*
Collins Ultimate Guide Rocks and Fossils by A. Busbey, R. Coenraads, D. Roots and P. Willis, HarperCollins*Publishers*

FAMILY: ELEMENT

ID FACT FILE

CRYSTAL SYSTEM:
Cubic

COLOR:
Copper-red

WHERE:
Hydrothermal

ABUNDANCE:
Common

FORM:
Cubic crystals, often twinned, or as thin sheets, threads or massive

CLEAVAGE:
None

HARDNESS:
2.5–3

SG:
8.9

LUSTER:
Metallic

TRANSPARENCY:
Opaque

TESTS:
Hackly fracture. Soft and malleable

LOOKALIKES:
None

Copper • Cu
Chemical group: Native element

Native copper occurs as a hydrothermal deposit associated with alteration of igneous and volcanic rocks, or infiltrating porous sedimentary rocks. It may occur in a specific enriched zone associated with a wide variety of additional copper minerals (oxides, sulfides, carbonates, etc.) in low-grade large-volume igneous "porphyry" copper deposits. It often contains minor amounts of other metals such as silver and bismuth.

FAMILY: ELEMENT

ID FACT FILE

CRYSTAL SYSTEM:
Cubic

COLOR:
White, colorless
or yellow; rarely
other colors

WHERE:
Metamorphic
mantle

ABUNDANCE:
Rare

FORM:
Equant
octahedral
crystals,
sometimes partly
rounded or
etched

CLEAVAGE:
One perfect
cleavage
direction

HARDNESS:
10

SG:
3.52

LUSTER:
Brilliant
adamantine

TRANSPARENCY:
Transparent

TESTS:
Hardest
known mineral.
High optical
dispersion

LOOKALIKES:
Various synthetic
gems of lower
hardness

Diamond • C

Chemical group: Native element

Diamond has unique physical properties. It
occurs at high pressure in the Earth's mantle in
coarse-grained metamorphic rocks such as
eclogite and garnet peridotite. Diamonds have
been transported periodically to the Earth's
surface by deep-sourced igneous volcanic
rocks, such as kimberlites and lamproites. They
are mined either from these host igneous
rocks, or from secondary placer deposits where
they have been secondarily concentrated. The
black variety of diamond known as *carbonado*
is a compact form of naturally sintered
diamond aggregate that is of industrial use.

FAMILY: ELEMENT

Gold • Au (impure)

Chemical group: Native element

ID FACT FILE

CRYSTAL SYSTEM:
Cubic

COLOR:
Yellow (gold)

WHERE:
Hydrothermal and alluvial

ABUNDANCE:
Rare

FORM:
Rare cubic crystals, usually flakes, rounded masses, "nuggets," or strings

CLEAVAGE:
None

HARDNESS:
2.5–3

SG:
12–20

LUSTER:
Metallic

TRANSPARENCY:
Opaque

TESTS:
Can be cut with a knife. Very high density (SG)

LOOKALIKES:
Pyrite cannot be cut with knife; chalcopyrite breaks beneath knife blade

Native gold is often alloyed with silver; the impurities vary with locality and may also include copper, iron, palladium, rhodium, etc. These affect the color; red tints result from copper and silver-rich gold is almost white. They also affect the physical properties; there is a large variation in density compared with pure elemental gold (SG = 18.7) reflecting substantial variations in impurities. The color, density, and malleability are distinctive. Chiefly exploited from reworked sedimentary placer deposits, the primary formation of gold is often related to hydrothermal veins associated with quartz. Additional associated minerals may include tellurides and sulfides. Gold is a siderophile (iron-loving) element and most of the Earth's gold budget should reside in the core. Gold is also slightly enriched in meteoritic iron.

FAMILY: ELEMENT

ID FACT FILE

Crystal system:
Hexagonal

Color:
Metal-gray

Where:
Hydrothermal
and metamorphic

Abundance:
Common

Form:
Usually massive;
platy crystals or
"scales"

Cleavage:
Easily cleaved

Hardness:
1–2

SG:
2–2.3

Luster:
Metallic

Transparency:
Opaque

Tests:
Black streak.
Cold to touch
due to high
thermal
conductivity

Lookalikes:
Molybdenite has
greenish-black
streak

Graphite • C

Chemical group: Native element

Graphite is widely distributed as a minor
component of metamorphic rocks, including
schists and gneisses. It is sometimes
concentrated in igneous hydrothermal veins
and pegmatites in contact metamorphic zones.
Where large deposits of high purity occur, it
has been mined and used for making pencils,
as in Ticonderoga, New York; Cumberland, in
England; Madagascar; and Sri Lanka.

FAMILY: ELEMENT

ID FACT FILE

CRYSTAL SYSTEM:
Liquid

COLOR:
Tin-white

WHERE:
Hydrothermal

ABUNDANCE:
Rare

FORM:
Liquid at room
temperature

CLEAVAGE:
None

HARDNESS:
<1

SG:
13.59

LUSTER:
Metallic

TRANSPARENCY:
Opaque

TESTS:
High density.
Distinctive
metallic liquid

LOOKALIKES:
None

Mercury • Hg

Chemical group: Native element

Native mercury or "quicksilver" is a silver-white
liquid at room temperature that vaporizes at
678°F (359°C). It may occur as droplets in cinnabar,
as at Almadén, Spain; Santa Cruz County,
California; and Idrija, Slovenia with which it
forms from hot springs by hydrothermal activity.
Mercury produces a vapor which is toxic; touch
and physical contact should be avoided.

FAMILY: ELEMENT

ID FACT FILE

CRYSTAL SYSTEM:
Cubic

COLOR:
White (silver)

WHERE:
Hydrothermal

ABUNDANCE:
Rare

FORM:
Distorted cubic crystals, string-like or massive

CLEAVAGE:
None

HARDNESS:
2.5–3

SG:
10.1–11.1

LUSTER:
Metallic

TRANSPARENCY:
Opaque

TESTS:
Hackly fracture. Soft and malleable

LOOKALIKES:
Silver-colored sulfides (arsenopyrite, marcasite, etc.) are brittle and much lower density

Silver • Ag (impure)

Chemical group: Native element

Native silver is usually slightly impure, with small amounts of alloyed metals, often including gold, copper, mercury, platinum, or bismuth; these additional components have a minor effect on the physical properties. It occurs in hydrothermal veins, often associated with quartz and sulfides including in particular argentite (Ag_2S), and may be secondarily concentrated in sedimentary placer deposits.

FAMILY: ELEMENT

ID FACT FILE

CRYSTAL SYSTEM:
Orthorhombic

COLOR:
Sulfur-yellow

WHERE:
Igneous

ABUNDANCE:
Common

FORM:
Crystalline with pyramidal terminations; massive or thin surface encrustations

CLEAVAGE:
Reasonable

HARDNESS:
1.5–2.5

SG:
2.07

LUSTER:
Resinous

TRANSPARENCY:
Transparent to opaque

TESTS:
Low density

LOOKALIKES:
None

Sulfur • S

Chemical group: Native element

Native sulfur is commonly deposited from volcanic gas emitted from active volcanoes; it is found in volcanic craters and in eroded remnants of volcanic structures. It is also formed as a hydrothermal deposit associated with hot springs. The color and low density are diagnostic. It may contain small amounts of selenium. Its bright yellow color is distinctive, both in crystals and surface coatings.

FAMILY: SULFIDE

ID FACT FILE

CRYSTAL SYSTEM:
Orthorhombic

COLOR:
Silver-white,
tarnishes

WHERE:
Igneous,
hydrothermal,
and metamorphic

ABUNDANCE:
Common

FORM:
Prismatic
crystals or
massive

CLEAVAGE:
Good

HARDNESS:
5.5–6

SG:
5.9–6.2

LUSTER:
Metallic

TRANSPARENCY:
Opaque

TESTS:
Uneven fracture.
Sparks when hit
with steel and
smells distinctly
of garlic

LOOKALIKES:
Silver is
malleable, and
lacks the garlic
smell when
struck.
Arsenopyrite
crystals
distinctive with
cleavage and
common twinning

Arsenopyrite • FeAsS

Chemical group: Sulfide

Arsenopyrite, once known as "mispickel," is a widespread hydrothermal sulfide often occurring in mixed sulfide veins (as in Cornwall, in England) together with tin, copper, cobalt, nickel, and especially lead and silver minerals. Native arsenic (As) also sometimes occurs. The hydrothermal veins are formed during the active cooling stages of large plutonic igneous rocks; mineralization was often developed along faulted contacts with metamorphic country rocks.

FAMILY: SULFIDE

ID FACT FILE

CRYSTAL SYSTEM:
Cubic (high temperature); tetragonal (low temperature)

COLOR:
Copper-red to brown, tarnished

WHERE:
Igneous, hydrothermal

ABUNDANCE:
Common

FORM:
Crystals may show cube or octahedron

CLEAVAGE:
Poor

HARDNESS:
3

SG:
4.9–5.4

LUSTER:
Metallic

TRANSPARENCY:
Opaque

TESTS:
Conchoidal to uneven fracture

LOOKALIKES:
None

Bornite • Cu_5FeS_4

Chemical group: Sulfide

Bornite is an important copper iron sulfide valued as a copper ore. Its particular red color when broken on fresh surfaces is distinctive; fresh surfaces develop an iridescent tarnish with tints of blue, green, and purple colors called "peacock." It occurs in pegmatites and hydrothermal veins often with quartz and chalcopyrite. Also dispersed in copper-rich bedded shales of Permian age in Germany.

FAMILY: SULFIDE

Chalcocite • Cu₂S

Chemical group: Sulfide

ID FACT FILE

CRYSTAL SYSTEM:
Orthorhombic

COLOR:
Black or gray;
subtle blue to
green tarnish

WHERE:
Hydrothermal
and metamorphic

ABUNDANCE:
Common

FORM:
Prismatic
crystals; massive
or granular

CLEAVAGE:
Good

HARDNESS:
2.5–3

SG:
5.5–5.8

LUSTER:
Metallic

TRANSPARENCY:
Opaque

TESTS:
Conchoidal
fracture. Lead-
gray streak.
Crystals often
twinned

LOOKALIKES:
None

Chalcocite, or "copper glance" as it is also known, is a simple copper sulfide. It usually occurs as a secondary alteration of original chalcopyrite or additional primary copper minerals. It can form in hydrothermal veins (as in Cornwall, in England). It often represents an important economic copper mineral in the secondary enriched zone of large porphyry copper deposits (as in Chuquicamata, in Chile; Butte, Montana). The photograph shows a cluster of tiny crystals greatly magnified.

ID FACT FILE

CRYSTAL SYSTEM:
Tetragonal

COLOR:
Brass-yellow, often tarnished

WHERE:
Igneous, hydrothermal and metamorphic

ABUNDANCE:
Common

FORM:
Crystals may show tetrahedral shapes; massive

CLEAVAGE:
Poor

HARDNESS:
3.5–4

SG:
4.1–4.3

LUSTER:
Metallic

TRANSPARENCY:
Opaque

TESTS:
Conchoidal to uneven fracture. Greenish-black streak

LOOKALIKES:
Tarnish resembles bornite, but broken fresh color diagnostic. Distinguished from gold by its brittle nature (and much lower density)

Chalcopyrite • $CuFeS_2$

Chemical group: Sulfide

Chalcopyrite, previously known as "copper pyrite," is one of the most important ore minerals for copper. Its particular brassy yellow color when broken on fresh surfaces is distinctive; these surfaces develop an iridescent tarnish similar to bornite. It forms chiefly as hydrothermal veins (as in Cornwall, in England), and as segregations in igneous rocks; it is also often associated with various contact metamorphic rocks.

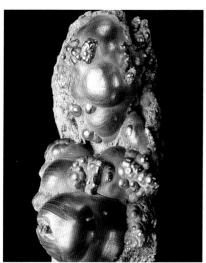

FAMILY: SULFIDE

ID FACT FILE

CRYSTAL SYSTEM:
Hexagonal

COLOR:
Bright vermilion red or brownish red

WHERE:
Igneous and hydrothermal

ABUNDANCE:
Restricted

FORM:
Tabular prismatic crystals; massive or granular

CLEAVAGE:
Good prismatic cleavage

HARDNESS:
2–2.5

SG:
8.1

LUSTER:
Adamantine or dull

TRANSPARENCY:
Opaque

TESTS:
Commonly associates with mercury

LOOKALIKES:
None

Cinnabar • HgS

Chemical group: Sulfide

Cinnabar, mercury sulfide, is formed by hydrothermal activity and hot springs related to volcanism, and is often associated with other sulfide minerals. At the famous locality in Almadén, in Spain, it occurs with iron, arsenic, and copper sulfides, in a quartzite host rock. Cinnabar has been used as a pigment.

FAMILY: COBALTITE

ID FACT FILE

CRYSTAL SYSTEM:
Cubic

COLOR:
Silver-white, reddish

WHERE:
Igneous and hydrothermal

ABUNDANCE:
Restricted

FORM:
Cubic crystals; massive or granular

CLEAVAGE:
Poor

HARDNESS:
5.5

SG:
6–6.3

LUSTER:
Metallic

TRANSPARENCY:
Opaque

TESTS:
Gray-black streak

LOOKALIKES:
None

Cobaltite • CoAsS

Chemical group: Sulfide

The sulfarsenide cobaltite occurs as a primary hydrothermal vein mineral. It often occurs with smaltite and silver, nickel, and copper minerals, plus gangue minerals of barite, calcite, and quartz, as at Cobalt, in Ontario, Canada. It can contain minor iron impurities. It is an important ore mineral of cobalt.

FAMILY: SULFIDE

ID FACT FILE

CRYSTAL SYSTEM:
Hexagonal

COLOR:
Indigo-blue

WHERE:
Hydrothermal

ABUNDANCE:
Common

FORM:
Platy hexagonal
crystals; massive

CLEAVAGE:
Distinctive basal
cleavage

HARDNESS:
1.5–2

SG:
4.6

LUSTER:
Metallic

TRANSPARENCY:
Opaque

TESTS:
Very soft, easily
scratched with
fingernail.
Distinctive blue
color

LOOKALIKES:
None

Covellite • CuS

Chemical group: Sulfide

Covellite is a typical secondary copper sulfide
mineral developed by relatively low-
temperature hydrothermal fluid alteration of
primary copper sulfides, such as chalcopyrite.
It is an important constituent of secondary
enriched layers in large porphyry copper
deposits, such as in Chuquicamata, in Chile.
Impurities may include iron and silver.

FAMILY: VIVIANITE

Erythrite • $Co_3(AsO_4)_2.8H_2O$

Chemical group: Arsenate

ID FACT FILE

CRYSTAL SYSTEM:
Monoclinic

COLOR:
Peach-red or crimson-red; rarely greenish

WHERE:
Hydrothermal

ABUNDANCE:
Restricted

FORM:
Earthy, encrusting of globular masses; prismatic crystals rare

CLEAVAGE:
Perfect

HARDNESS:
1.5–2.5

SG:
3.1

LUSTER:
Pearly; dull when massive

TRANSPARENCY:
Transparent to translucent

TESTS:
Reddish streak. The streak powder is lavender-blue

LOOKALIKES:
Cuprite

The characteristic color of erythrite, also known as "cobalt bloom," makes it a useful pathfinder to locate cobalt-rich mineral deposits as at Cobalt, in Ontario, Canada and Bou Azzer, in Morocco. It occurs as a secondary oxidation or weathering product of primary cobalt minerals, such as cobaltite. Impurities include calcium, nickel and iron.

FAMILY: SULFIDE

ID FACT FILE

CRYSTAL SYSTEM:
Cubic

COLOR:
Lead-gray

WHERE:
Hydrothermal

ABUNDANCE:
Common

FORM:
Cubic crystals;
massive

CLEAVAGE:
Good cleavage
parallel to cube
faces

HARDNESS:
2.5

SG:
7.4–7.6

LUSTER:
Metallic; dull
tarnish

TRANSPARENCY:
Opaque

TESTS:
Even fracture.
Lead-gray streak

LOOKALIKES:
Antimony
sulfides. The
leadlike color of
galena combined
with its
propensity to
form cube-
shaped crystals
is diagnostic

Galena • PbS

Chemical group: Sulfide

Galena has been one of the most important ore
minerals for lead since Roman times. It is
formed by hydrothermal fluids often related to
igneous heat sources from cooling plutons.
Galena may contain impurities that are
important in themselves. Thus, "argentiferous
galena" contains significant amounts of silver;
galena may also contain zinc, iron, copper,
antimony, bismuth, and even trace levels of
gold. Selenium may substitute for sulfur. It
frequently occurs together with sphalerite.

FAMILY: COMPLEX SULFIDE

Jamesonite •
$Pb_4FeSb_6S_{14}$

Chemical group: Sulfide

Jamesonite is one of several complex sulfides
of antimony (Sb). It is formed by hydrothermal
fluids and frequently occurs in veins associated
with other antimony-bearing sulfides, and
lead-silver- or copper-rich complex antimony-
sulfides, as in Cornwall, in England.

ID FACT FILE

CRYSTAL SYSTEM:
Monoclinic

COLOR:
Dark lead-gray

WHERE:
Hydrothermal

ABUNDANCE:
Restricted

FORM:
Elongated,
acicular crystals,
often feathery;
massive

CLEAVAGE:
Clear basal
cleavage

HARDNESS:
2–3

SG:
5.5–6

LUSTER:
Metallic

TRANSPARENCY:
Opaque

TESTS:
Dark gray-black
streak

LOOKALIKES:
Crystal shapes
are distinctive;
massive forms
are darker gray
than galena

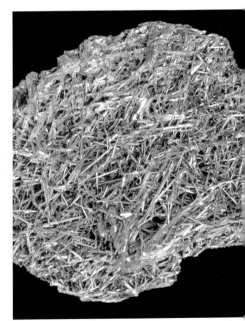

FAMILY: IRON ARSENIDE

ID FACT FILE

CRYSTAL SYSTEM:
Orthorhombic

COLOR:
Silver-white,
tarnishes gray

WHERE:
Hydrothermal

ABUNDANCE:
Restricted

FORM:
Prismatic
crystals;
disseminated

CLEAVAGE:
Perfect

HARDNESS:
5–5.5

SG:
7.1–7.5

LUSTER:
Metallic

TRANSPARENCY:
Opaque

TESTS:
Uneven, brittle
fracture. Gray-
black streak

LOOKALIKES:
Arsenopyrite

Löllingite • $FeAs_2$

Chemical group: Arsenide

Löllingite occurs as a primary hydrothermal
mineral in mixed sulfide-arsenic vein systems,
usually in minor amounts, as in Lölling, in
Germany. The shiny metallic luster of fresh
broken surfaces contrasts with the dull gray
tarnish of weathered surfaces.

FAMILY: MARCASITE

ID FACT FILE

CRYSTAL SYSTEM:
Orthorhombic

COLOR:
Pale bronze-yellow to almost white

WHERE:
Hydrothermal

ABUNDANCE:
Common

FORM:
Crystals commonly tabular and twinned giving cockscomb and spear-shaped groups; also radiating aggregates

CLEAVAGE:
Good

HARDNESS:
6–6.5

SG:
4.9

LUSTER:
Metallic

TRANSPARENCY:
Opaque

TESTS:
Grayish streak. Uneven fracture, brittle

LOOKALIKES:
It is paler in color than pyrite

Marcasite • FeS_2

Chemical group: Sulfide

Marcasite is the low-temperature polymorph of pyrite and occurs commonly as a secondary mineral forming concretions in sedimentary rocks where its spherulitic form of radiating crystals is distinctive. It may form by precipitation from low-temperature hydrothermal fluids.

FAMILY: SULFIDE

ID FACT FILE

CRYSTAL SYSTEM:
Hexagonal

COLOR:
Lead-gray

WHERE:
Hydrothermal

ABUNDANCE:
Common

FORM:
Usually forms scales, platy crystals; or massive

CLEAVAGE:
Good

HARDNESS:
1–1.5

SG:
4.7–4.8

LUSTER:
Metallic

TRANSPARENCY:
Opaque

TESTS:
Greenish-gray streak. Sectile and almost malleable

LOOKALIKES:
Greenish streak distinguishes molybdenite from graphite

Molybdenite • MoS_2

Chemical group: Sulfide

Small amounts of molybdenite occur in acid igneous rocks such as granites and granitic pegmatites. It also occurs in contact metamorphic zones adjacent to granitic intrusions. Its form of bright gray scaly crystals is often distinctive and it is further distinguished by its physical properties including the ability to be "flaked" with a fingernail. May contain selenium.

FAMILY: ARSENIC SULFIDE

Orpiment • As_2S_3

Chemical group: Sulfide

ID FACT FILE

CRYSTAL SYSTEM:
Monoclinic

COLOR:
Lemon-yellow, orange

WHERE:
Igneous, hydrothermal/ sublimate

ABUNDANCE:
Restricted

FORM:
Rare prismatic crystals; massive

CLEAVAGE:
Perfect

HARDNESS:
1.5–2

SG:
3.4–3.5

LUSTER:
Pearly on cleaved surfaces, resinous to dull if massive

TRANSPARENCY:
Translucent

TESTS:
Yellow

LOOKALIKES:
Sulfur

Orpiment is a simple arsenic sulfide formed as a hydrothermal deposit or as a sublimate condensed from hot volcanic gas. It is often associated with realgar, another arsenic sulfide, and with the more oxidized levels of arsenic mineral-rich veins. Its color and physical properties are diagnostic. It can form an encrusting sublimate from volcanic gas, as in Naples, in Italy and Humboldt County, Nevada.

FAMILY: PENTLANDITE

ID FACT FILE

CRYSTAL SYSTEM:
Cubic

COLOR:
Bronze-yellow

WHERE:
Igneous,
hydrothermal

ABUNDANCE:
Common

FORM:
Usually massive

CLEAVAGE:
Poor

HARDNESS:
3.5–4

SG:
5.0

LUSTER:
Metallic

TRANSPARENCY:
Opaque

TESTS:
Uneven fracture

LOOKALIKES:
Other sulfides
mainly
distinguished by
color

Pentlandite • $(Fe,Ni)_9S_8$

Chemical group: Sulfide

Pentlandite is an important economic mineral for nickel. It occurs in association with pyrrhotite and other Ni-minerals in deposits in Broken Hill, in Australia; Espedalen, in Norway; and in the impact-formed Sudbury Complex, in Ontario, Canada. It contains some cobalt.

It oxidizes to a variety of secondary nickel minerals, including millerite and niccolite. Pentlandite is also a minor secondary mineral in iron meteorites.

FAMILY: PYRITE

ID FACT FILE

CRYSTAL SYSTEM:
Cubic

COLOR:
Bronze-yellow to
pale brass-yellow

WHERE:
Igneous,
hydrothermal

ABUNDANCE:
Very common

FORM:
Cube,
pyritohedron;
often massive

CLEAVAGE:
Cube faces are
often strongly
striated

HARDNESS:
6–6.5

SG:
4.8–5.1

LUSTER:
Metallic

TRANSPARENCY:
Opaque

TESTS:
Conchoidal or
uneven fracture.
Makes sparks
when struck with
steel. Streak
greenish or
brownish black

LOOKALIKES:
Chalcopyrite and
other sulfides
distinguished by
physical
properties

Pyrite • FeS_2

Chemical group: Sulfide

Pyrite, or "fool's gold," occurs chiefly as a
primary mineral in hydrothermal vein systems,
and as a low-temperature product in igneous
rocks, including active volcanic systems. It is
widely distributed in all types of rocks as a
secondary mineral; it may for example replace
fossils in sedimentary rocks. The form and
striations on the faces of pyrite crystals are
diagnostic. It may contain minor amounts of
copper or trace amounts of gold.

FAMILY: SULFIDE

Pyrrhotite • FeS

Chemical group: Sulfide

Pyrrhotite is an iron sulfide that often
contains some nickel (up to about 5 per cent),
for which it is exploited. In the largest known
nickel deposit at Sudbury/Canada, it forms
huge ore-bodies together with pentlandite; it
probably formed as magmatic segregations
from an igneous norite and also involved hydrothermal activity. It is also found in typical
hydrothermal vein deposits as in Cornwall,
England and Norway. The photograph shows
rare crystals.

FAMILY: SULFIDE

ID FACT FILE

CRYSTAL SYSTEM:
Monoclinic

COLOR:
Red to orange

WHERE:
Igneous,
hydrothermal/
sublimate

ABUNDANCE:
Restricted

FORM:
Rare prismatic
crystals;
massive,
granular

CLEAVAGE:
Poor

HARDNESS:
2

SG:
4.5–4.6

LUSTER:
Resinous

TRANSPARENCY:
Translucent

TESTS:
Red-orange
streak

LOOKALIKES:
None

Realgar • As_2S_2

Chemical group: Sulfide

Realgar is simple arsenic sulfide formed as a hydrothermal deposit or as a sublimate condensed from hot volcanic gas. It is often associated with orpiment, another arsenic sulfide, or with cinnabar as in Spain. Its color and physical properties are diagnostic. Native arsenic (SG = 5.7) also very occasionally occurs, and is recognized by its brittle fracture, steel-gray color, and brilliant luster.

ID FACT FILE

CRYSTAL SYSTEM:
Cubic

COLOR:
Yellowish brown or black; occasionally yellow or white

WHERE:
Igneous, hydrothermal

ABUNDANCE:
Very common

FORM:
Crystals usually tetrahedra or rhombododeca-hedra; massive

CLEAVAGE:
Good

HARDNESS:
3.5–4

SG:
3.9–4.2

LUSTER:
Resinous to adamantine

TRANSPARENCY:
Translucent to transparent

TESTS:
Conchoidal fracture; brittle. Streak white to yellow and brown

LOOKALIKES:
None

Sphalerite • ZnS

Chemical group: Sulfide

Sphalerite is probably the most common zinc mineral and forms in hydrothermal vein systems of various types often with galena and other sulfides, as for example in Cornwall, in England and in Joplin, Kansas. Almost all sphalerite has some iron; other impurities may include arsenic, mercury, iron and cadmium.

FAMILY: STANNITE

ID FACT FILE

CRYSTAL SYSTEM:
Tetragonal

COLOR:
Gray to bronze or yellowish; tarnishes

WHERE:
Hydrothermal

ABUNDANCE:
Restricted

FORM:
Usually massive, granular; rare crystals

CLEAVAGE:
Poor

HARDNESS:
4

SG:
4.4

LUSTER:
Metallic

TRANSPARENCY:
Opaque

TESTS:
Blackish streak

LOOKALIKES:
Cassiterite

Stannite • Cu_2FeSnS_4

Chemical group: Sulfide

Stannite is a complex sulfide of tin, copper, and iron and often contains minor zinc in addition. It is an important source of tin, and often occurs in hydrothermal deposits with cassiterite and other iron, copper, silver, and arsenic minerals. It may also contain traces of germanium.

FAMILY: ANTIMONY SULFIDE

ID FACT FILE

CRYSTAL SYSTEM:
Orthorhombic

COLOR:
Lead-gray

WHERE:
Hydrothermal

ABUNDANCE:
Restricted

FORM:
Elongated
crystals, bladed,
sheaves; crystals
may be curved

CLEAVAGE:
Good

HARDNESS:
2

SG:
4.5–4.6

LUSTER:
Metallic

TRANSPARENCY:
Opaque

TESTS:
Lead-gray streak.
Lower density
than galena.
Subconchoidal or
brittle fracture

LOOKALIKES:
Crystal shapes
are distinctive;
massive forms
are darker gray
than galena

Stibnite • Sb_2S_3

Chemical group: Sulfide

Stibnite is the simple trisulfide of antimony
(Sb). It is formed by hydrothermal fluids
and frequently occurs in quartz-stibnite veins
but also occurs with quartz, dolomite, calcite,
and barite in "white" veins as in Cornwall, in
England and in Lengshuijang, in China.
Antimony rarely occurs as the native element,
and stibnite is perhaps the most important
economic primary mineral of antimony.

Tennantite •
$(Cu,Fe)_{12}As_4S_{13}$

Chemical group: Arsenic-sulfide

ID FACT FILE

CRYSTAL SYSTEM:
Cubic

COLOR:
Gray with olive tint

WHERE:
Hydrothermal

ABUNDANCE:
Restricted

FORM:
Well-shaped crystals (tetrahedra); granular or dense aggregates

CLEAVAGE:
None

HARDNESS:
3–4.5

SG:
4.6–4.8

LUSTER:
Metallic-dull

TRANSPARENCY:
Opaque; very thin splinters are reddish

TESTS:
Conchoidal brittle fracture. Black to reddish brown streak

LOOKALIKES:
Tetrahedrite

Usually occurs as a massive or encrusting dark gray mineral. Well formed crystals may show distinctive triangular (tetrahedral) faces in many ways like tetrahedrite (*see* p.42). It is found in copper- and lead-bearing hydrothermal vein systems, associated with tetrahedrite, siderite, galena, and sphalerite, as in Cornwall, in England, Harz in Germany, Boliden in Sweden, and Alsace in France.

FAMILY: TETRAHEDRITE

Tetrahedrite • $(Cu,Fe)_{12}Sb_4S_{13}$

Chemical group: Antimony-sulfide

ID FACT FILE

CRYSTAL SYSTEM:
Cubic

COLOR:
Gray with olive tint

WHERE:
Hydrothermal

ABUNDANCE:
Restricted

FORM:
Well shaped crystals (tetrahedra); granular or dense aggregates

CLEAVAGE:
None

HARDNESS:
3–4

SG:
4.6–5.2

LUSTER:
Metallic-dull

TRANSPARENCY:
Opaque; very thin splinters are reddish

TESTS:
Conchoidal brittle fracture. Black to brown streak

LOOKALIKES:
Tennantite

Tetrahedrite occurs in copper- and lead-bearing hydrothermal vein systems, associated with siderite, galena, and sphalerite, as in Cornwall, in England; Harz, in Germany; and Lima, in Peru. Impurities are often economically important and can include iron, silver, zinc, gold, or mercury. Crystals are usually very distinctive with four triangular faces (tetrahedra), sometimes twinned.

FAMILY: FLUORIDE

ID FACT FILE

CRYSTAL SYSTEM:
Cubic

COLOR:
Variable;
colorless, white,
green, purple,
blue, or yellow

WHERE:
Hydrothermal,
igneous

ABUNDANCE:
Common

FORM:
Common cube
crystals, rarely
other shapes;
also granular

CLEAVAGE:
Perfect
(octahedral)

HARDNESS:
4

SG:
3–3.25

LUSTER:
Vitreous

TRANSPARENCY:
Transparent to
translucent

TESTS:
Conchoidal to
uneven fracture;
brittle. Crystals
may be
concentrically
zoned in color

LOOKALIKES:
Colored fluorite
"cubes" are
unlikely to be
mistaken

Fluorite • CaF_2

Chemical group: Halide

Fluorite is formed by hydrothermal fluids and usually occurs in vein systems related to large igneous bodies; it is often associated with sphalerite, galena, barite, and quartz, as in the Pennines, in England. It can also occur as a primary mineral in some alkaline igneous rocks, such as syenite pegmatites and carbonatites. Displays a wide variety of colors and may be zoned; very distinctive cubes.

FAMILY: CHLORIDE

ID FACT FILE

CRYSTAL SYSTEM:
Cubic

COLOR:
Colorless, white, yellow, red

WHERE:
Sedimentary

ABUNDANCE:
Abundant

FORM:
Common cube crystals; also massive

CLEAVAGE:
Perfect

HARDNESS:
2–2.5

SG:
2.2

LUSTER:
Vitreous

TRANSPARENCY:
Transparent to translucent

TESTS:
Tastes saline (test not recommended). Soluble in water

LOOKALIKES:
Sylvite, KCl, tastes more bitter and crystals can show octahedral faces

Halite • NaCl

Chemical group: Halide

Halite forms by evaporation of saline bodies of water, such as sabkhas. Substantial bedded deposits of "rock salt" occur throughout the stratigraphic record, including in the Permian in Germany, Trias in Cheshire, in England and in more recent years, Searles Lake, California. Halite can occur with a variety of additional evaporite minerals, such as complex sulfates and carbonates of calcium, magnesium, and potassium; sylvite, KCl, is the potassium equivalent of halite.

FAMILY: CHLORIDE

Sylvite • KCl

Chemical group: Halide

ID FACT FILE

CRYSTAL SYSTEM:
Cubic

COLOR:
Colorless or white

WHERE:
Sedimentary, volcanic

ABUNDANCE:
Abundant

FORM:
Common cube crystals; also granular

CLEAVAGE:
Perfect

HARDNESS:
1.5–2

SG:
2.0

LUSTER:
Vitreous, greasy

TRANSPARENCY:
Transparent to translucent

TESTS:
Uneven, brittle fracture. Tastes bitter (test not recommended). Soluble in water

LOOKALIKES:
Halite. KCl tastes more bitter and crystals can show octahedral faces

Sylvite occurs in evaporite and potash salt deposits. It is usually associated with halite and other chlorides (*see* halite p.44). Sylvite tastes more bitter than halite and crystals may have small additional corner faces (triangular). Tends to be hygroscopic (attracts water) and softer than halite. Also occurs as volcanic sublimate, as in Mt. Vesuvius, in Italy. Common constituent of desiccating hyper-alkaline lakes, as in Chilean Andes in Calama.

FAMILY: TIN OXIDE

ID FACT FILE

CRYSTAL SYSTEM:
Tetragonal

COLOR:
Black, brown,
yellow or reddish

WHERE:
Hydrothermal,
igneous, placers

ABUNDANCE:
Common

FORM:
Squat terminated
prisms; also
fibrous or
massive

CLEAVAGE:
Reasonable

HARDNESS:
7

SG:
6.6–7.1

LUSTER:
Adamantine,
greasy

TRANSPARENCY:
Transparent to
opaque

TESTS:
Conchoidal,
brittle. White,
brownish streak

LOOKALIKES:
Zircon

Cassiterite • SnO_2

Chemical group: Oxide

Cassiterite (*tinstone*) occurs in hydrothermal
vein systems often with abundant quartz
associated with boron or fluorine minerals
(fluorite, tourmaline, axinite, etc.). It also
occurs in granite pegmatites and in
metasomatized granites called "greisens" or
adjacent metamorphosed country rocks.
Cassiterite occurs in secondary placer deposits,
which are often of economic value. Formerly
an important ore mineral for the tin industry.

ID FACT FILE

CRYSTAL SYSTEM:
Hexagonal

COLOR:
Gray, green, red, blue, yellow

WHERE:
Igneous, metamorphic, placers

ABUNDANCE:
Common

FORM:
Barrel-shaped or pointed prisms; also fibrous or massive

CLEAVAGE:
None

HARDNESS:
9

SG:
4–4.1

LUSTER:
Vitreous

TRANSPARENCY:
Transparent to opaque

TESTS:
Conchoidal, splintery, brittle. White streak

LOOKALIKES:
Hardness is unlikely to be mistaken

Corundum • Al_2O_3

Chemical group: Oxide

Corundum occurs as a primary mineral in igneous and metamorphic rocks. It is the second-hardest mineral known. Common varieties are cloudy. Clear varieties are used to make gemstones. *Ruby* is red and occurs in marble, schist, and placer deposits. *Sapphire* refers to all colored gem varieties that are not red, including pink, blue, or yellow varieties, and occurs in contact metamorphic rocks, in placers and in some igneous rocks, as in Thailand and the state of Montana.

ID FACT FILE

CRYSTAL SYSTEM:
Cubic

COLOR:
Red shades

WHERE:
Hydrothermal

ABUNDANCE:
Restricted

FORM:
Crystals often small octahedra; also massive, granular

CLEAVAGE:
Perfect

HARDNESS:
3.5–4

SG:
5.8–6.2

LUSTER:
Metallic, dull

TRANSPARENCY:
Translucent to opaque

TESTS:
Conchoidal, uneven, brittle. Brown-red streak

LOOKALIKES:
Crocoite, limonite

Cuprite • Cu_2O

Chemical group: Oxide

Cuprite, simple copper oxide, is a typical secondary copper mineral formed in the oxidized zones of hydrothermal and porphyry copper deposits. It often forms from the breakdown of primary sulfides of copper; it may be associated with native copper, and iron oxides such as limonite.

FAMILY: ALUMINUM HYDROXIDE

ID FACT FILE

CRYSTAL SYSTEM:
Orthorhombic

COLOR:
Colorless, white

WHERE:
Sedimentary,
metamorphic

ABUNDANCE:
Abundant

FORM:
Small tabular
crystals rare;
lamellar
aggregates,
massive

CLEAVAGE:
Perfect

HARDNESS:
6.5–7

SG:
3.3–3.5

LUSTER:
Vitreous to pearly

TRANSPARENCY:
Transparent to
translucent

TESTS:
Conchoidal,
brittle. White
streak

LOOKALIKES:
Mixed Al-
hydroxides in
bauxite

Diaspore • AlOOH

Chemical group: Hydroxide

Diaspore occurs with other hydroxides of
aluminum, such as gibbsite, in the red-brown
tropical weathering product of silicate rocks
called bauxite. *Bauxite* is an important
economic ore for aluminum, as in Brazil.
Diaspore is also a secondary mineral with
corundum in metamorphic rocks.

FAMILY: IRON OXIDE

ID FACT FILE

CRYSTAL SYSTEM:
Hexagonal-
trigonal

COLOR:
Black, gray, red-
brown

WHERE:
Igneous,
sedimentary,
metamorphic

ABUNDANCE:
Abundant

FORM:
Chunky to platy
crystals;
granular,
radiating, and
globular

CLEAVAGE:
None

HARDNESS:
6–6.5

SG:
4.9–5.3

LUSTER:
Metallic, dull

TRANSPARENCY:
Opaque except
very thin flakes
blood-red

TESTS:
Conchoidal,
brittle. Cherry-red
streak

LOOKALIKES:
Pyrolusite,
psilomelane

Hematite • Fe_2O_3

Chemical group: Oxide

Hematite occurs widely in a variety of forms in
different rocks. "Kidney ore" is massive with a
distinctive globular surface and internal
radiating structure. "Specular iron" consists of
abundant shiny metallic hematite crystals.
"Reddle" is earthy hematite used as a pigment
and a polish. "Micaceous iron" is thin lamellar
hematite crystals. An important ore mineral for
iron, it has been mined in Cumberland, in
England; Elba, in Italy; Bilbao, in Spain; Bahia,
in Brazil; and in many other countries.

FAMILY: IRON TITANIUM OXIDE

ID FACT FILE

CRYSTAL SYSTEM:
Trigonal

COLOR:
Black tinted violet

WHERE:
Igneous, sedimentary

ABUNDANCE:
Common

FORM:
Tabular to platy crystals; granular aggregates or dispersed

CLEAVAGE:
None

HARDNESS:
5–6

SG:
4.5–5

LUSTER:
Metallic, dull

TRANSPARENCY:
Opaque

TESTS:
Conchoidal, brittle. Brown-black streak

LOOKALIKES:
Iron oxides

Ilmenite • FeTiO$_3$

Chemical group: Oxide

Ilmenite occurs widely in small quantities in igneous rocks like gabbros; sometimes large accumulations are important for titanium and have been mined in Norway, Sweden, and in the Southern Urals, in Russia. It is more resistant to weathering than pure iron oxides and can form economic deposits in beach sands, as in India and Australia. Impurities can include magnesia and admixtures of other iron oxides, with which it is often associated.

FAMILY: SPINEL

Magnetite • Fe_3O_4

Chemical group: Oxide

ID FACT FILE

CRYSTAL SYSTEM:
Cubic

COLOR:
Black

WHERE:
Igneous,
sedimentary,
metamorphic

ABUNDANCE:
Abundant

FORM:
Equant well
formed crystals;
granular
aggregates

CLEAVAGE:
Imperfect

HARDNESS:
5.5

SG:
5.2

LUSTER:
Metallic, dull

TRANSPARENCY:
Opaque

TESTS:
Conchoidal,
brittle. Black
streak. Strongly
magnetic

LOOKALIKES:
Iron oxides,
chromite

Magnetite occurs in small quantities in most igneous rocks; sometimes large accumulations are economic as in Sweden, Finland, and in the Urals in Russia. It also occurs in metamorphic skarn, in schist and in "black sand" placer deposits. Impurities include magnesia and titanium. It is the most widespread economic ore of iron. Strong crystal shapes (octahedra) even for very small crystals, are typical. Magnetic properties cause a compass needle to swing. Variety titanomagnetite contains titanium. Photo shows magnetic properties with straight pins.

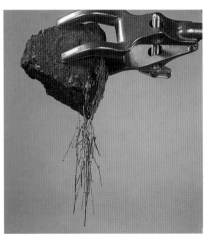

ID FACT FILE

CRYSTAL SYSTEM:
Orthorhombic

COLOR:
Brown, black,
occasionally
yellow

WHERE:
Igneous

ABUNDANCE:
Common

FORM:
Stubby crystals,
prismatic;
granular
dispersed

CLEAVAGE:
Good

HARDNESS:
5.5

SG:
4.0–4.8

LUSTER:
Metallic, greasy

TRANSPARENCY:
Transparent to
opaque

TESTS:
Conchoidal,
brittle fracture.
White streak

LOOKALIKES:
Spinel,
pyrochlore,
melanite

Perovskite • $CaTiO_3$

Chemical group: Titanate

Perovskite is a common accessory mineral in alkaline igneous rocks, including nephelinite, ijolite, pegmatite, and carbonatite. Impurities include the rare earth elements, zirconium and niobium. Usually forms small granular crystals distinguished from otherwise similar pyrochlore by streak test. Perovskite is also stable at high pressure and usually present in small amounts in igneous rocks from greatest depth such as kimberlite. A magnesium silicate variety of perovskite with similar structure is thought to be the most abundant mineral in the Earth's lower mantle.

ID FACT FILE

CRYSTAL SYSTEM:
Cubic

COLOR:
Brown, black,
occasionally
yellow

WHERE:
Igneous

ABUNDANCE:
Common

FORM:
Good crystals,
cubes, or 8-sided
(octahedra);
massive

CLEAVAGE:
None

HARDNESS:
5–5.5

SG:
3.5–4.6

LUSTER:
Adamantine,
greasy

TRANSPARENCY:
Opaque to
translucent

TESTS:
Conchoidal,
uneven, brittle
fracture. Yellow-
brown streak

LOOKALIKES:
Spinel, melanite

Pyrochlore • $(Na,Ca)_2$ $(Nb,Ta)_2O_6(O,OH,F)$

Chemical group: Oxide

Pyrochlore is a common accessory mineral in
alkaline igneous rocks, including pegmatites
and carbonatites. Impurities include the rare
earth elements, uranium and thorium.
Niobium-rich varieties may be pale in color or
yellow. The niobium is often partly replaced
by tantalum; the pure tantalum variety is
called microlite. Forms economic deposits for
niobium and tantalum concentrated by
weathering of carbonatites, as in Brazil and in
East Africa.

FAMILY: MANGANESE DIOXIDE

ID FACT FILE

CRYSTAL SYSTEM:
Tetragonal

COLOR:
Black, gray

WHERE:
Sedimentary,
hydrothermal

ABUNDANCE:
Common

FORM:
Massive,
globular or
radiating; small
crystals rare

CLEAVAGE:
Perfect

HARDNESS:
Crystals 6.5,
massive 2–6

SG:
4.7

LUSTER:
Metallic, dull

TRANSPARENCY:
Opaque

TESTS:
Uneven, brittle
fracture. Black
streak. Often
slightly stains
hands

LOOKALIKES:
Hematite,
romanechite

Pyrolusite • MnO_2

Chemical group: Oxide

Pyrolusite is a chief source of manganese and
occurs in sedimentary rocks either as
precipitates with iron, or by weathering and
replacing of manganese-bearing minerals,
typically silicates. This can result in aggregates,
nodules, and layers with clays, such as laterites
in Brazil and India. The photograph shows rare
small crystals (enlarged).

FAMILY: PSILOMELANE

Romanechite •
$(Ba, H_2O)_2Mn_5O_{10}$

Chemical group: Oxide

Romanechite (previously called psilomelane) is
one of several manganese oxides belonging to
the psilomelane group, which are manganese
oxide minerals containing some structural water
(hydrous). It occurs as a secondary mineral in the
oxidation zone of hydrothermal manganese ore
deposits. Often associated with pyrolusite, as in
Cornwall, in England; Saxony and the Black
Forest, in Germany; and Romaneche, in France.
Impurities may include some iron and potassium.

ID FACT FILE

CRYSTAL SYSTEM:
Monoclinic

COLOR:
Black, gray

WHERE:
Hydrothermal

ABUNDANCE:
Restricted

FORM:
Massive,
globular or
stalactitic;
crystals rare

CLEAVAGE:
None

HARDNESS:
5–6

SG:
4.7

LUSTER:
Metallic, dull

TRANSPARENCY:
Opaque

TESTS:
Uneven, brittle
fracture. Black-
brown streak

LOOKALIKES:
Hematite,
pyrolusite

FAMILY: TITANIUM OXIDE

ID FACT FILE

CRYSTAL SYSTEM:
Tetragonal

COLOR:
Red, brown, yellow, black

WHERE:
Igneous, metamorphic

ABUNDANCE:
Common

FORM:
Elongated crystals, needles or twinned larger crystals; massive granular

CLEAVAGE:
Poor

HARDNESS:
6–6.5

SG:
4.2

LUSTER:
Adamantine, metallic

TRANSPARENCY:
Transparent to opaque

TESTS:
Conchoidal, uneven, brittle fracture. Yellowish-brown streak

LOOKALIKES:
None

Rutile • TiO_2

Chemical group: Oxide

Rutile is the simple oxide of titanium and is an important source of titanium. It is a widespread minor constituent of igneous rocks such as granites, diorites, and pegmatites. It also occurs in metamorphic gneisses and amphibolites. May be concentrated by secondary weathering into economic beach sand deposits as in Australia, South Africa, and Florida. It also occurs as fine fibrous needles distributed through quartz crystals called "rutilated quartz." The photograph shows a small well formed crystal much enlarged.

ID FACT FILE

CRYSTAL SYSTEM:
Cubic

COLOR:
All colors,
commonly red,
black, brown

WHERE:
Igneous,
metamorphic

ABUNDANCE:
Common

FORM:
Well formed
crystals
(octahedra)

CLEAVAGE:
Imperfect

HARDNESS:
8

SG:
3.5–4.1

LUSTER:
Vitreous

TRANSPARENCY:
Transparent to
opaque

TESTS:
Conchoidal,
brittle fracture.
White streak

LOOKALIKES:
Garnet,
pyrochlore

Spinel • $MgAl_2O_4$

Chemical group: Oxide

Spinel is one member of a family of spinels
with large ranges in composition; most spinel
contains some chromium, iron, and manganese.
It occurs in igneous rocks like basalt, gabbro,
and peridotite, and in metamorphic rocks like
schists, hornfels, and marble. Colored varieties
(especially blue and red) used for gems occur
in placer deposits as in Thailand and Myanmar.
Varieties include black-colored *hercynite*
($FeAl_2O_4$), and *chromite* ($FeCr_2O_4$). Igneous
chromite concentrations are mined for
chromium, as in South Africa.

FAMILY: URANIUM OXIDE

ID FACT FILE

Crystal system:
Cubic

Color:
Black

Where:
Igneous,
hydrothermal

Abundance:
Uncommon

Form:
Crystals small
cubes or
octahedra; also
massive

Cleavage:
None

Hardness:
4–6

SG:
9.1–10.6

Luster:
Greasy, dull

Transparency:
Opaque

Tests:
Conchoidal,
uneven fracture.
Black, greenish
streak. Strongly
radioactive

Lookalikes:
Radioactivity and
high density
unlikely to be
mistaken

Uraninite • UO_2

Chemical group: Oxide

Uraninite (old name "pitchblende") is often impure, containing some thorium, zirconium, and lead. It occurs as a primary mineral in igneous rocks like granites and pegmatites; also in hydrothermal vein systems with lead, copper, and tin minerals as in Cornwall, in England; Saxony, in Germany; and in the state of New Hampshire. It is an important source of uranium. In addition to the normal physical tests, uraninite is strongly radioactive; it can be detected with a geiger counter and is a serious health hazard.

FAMILY: APATITE

ID FACT FILE

CRYSTAL SYSTEM:
Hexagonal

COLOR:
Ruby-red, orange-brown, or yellowish

WHERE:
Hydrothermal

ABUNDANCE:
Restricted

FORM:
Stubby prismatic crystals; sometimes encrusting

CLEAVAGE:
None

HARDNESS:
3

SG:
6.5–7.1

LUSTER:
Adamantine, greasy

TRANSPARENCY:
Opaque

TESTS:
Conchoidal, brittle fracture. Pale yellow streak

LOOKALIKES:
Pyromorphite, crocoite, cuprite

Vanadinite • $Pb_5(VO_4)_3Cl$

Chemical group: Vanadate

Vanadinite is a lead vanadate mineral usually with a distinctive bright reddish color. It often contains some phosphorous and arsenic. It occurs as a secondary mineral in the oxidation zone of hydrothermal lead vein systems, as in Namibia, in Zambia, and in Arizona. Often associated with other oxidized lead minerals such as pyromorphite; it is sometimes an economic source of vanadium. The photograph shows clusters of small crystals much enlarged.

FAMILY: WOLFRAMITE

Wolframite •
$(Fe,Mn)WO_4$

Chemical group: Tungstate

ID FACT FILE

CRYSTAL SYSTEM:
Monoclinic

COLOR:
Brown-black

WHERE:
Hydrothermal

ABUNDANCE:
Restricted

FORM:
Tabular crystals,
bladed or
massive

CLEAVAGE:
Perfect

HARDNESS:
5–5.5

SG:
7.1–7.6

LUSTER:
Metallic to dull

TRANSPARENCY:
Transparent to
opaque

TESTS:
Uneven fracture.
Chocolate-brown
streak

LOOKALIKES:
Ilmenite

Wolframite is a simple iron tungstate with some additional manganese. It occurs in hydrothermal vein systems associated with tin minerals and quartz as in Cornwall, in England and in Bolivia. It is the most important ore mineral for tungsten (W). The precise amount of iron and manganese varies considerably, and it may contain some calcium. Wolframite derived from tungsten-tin veins also forms economic sedimentary placer deposits, as in Myanmar.

FAMILY: CARBONATE

Ankerite •
$Ca(Fe,Mg)(CO_3)_2$

Chemical group: Carbonate

Ankerite is the uncommon iron-rich equivalent of dolomite. It occurs in sedimentary rocks modified by iron-rich mineralization, or where iron is otherwise abundant. It also occurs as a primary mineral in rare iron-rich varieties of igneous carbonate rocks, such as iron-rich carbonatites. It often forms well shaped crystals with slightly curved faces and often resembles a brown-colored form of dolomite.

ID FACT FILE

CRYSTAL SYSTEM:
Trigonal

COLOR:
White to brown

WHERE:
Sedimentary, igneous

ABUNDANCE:
Uncommon

FORM:
Well shaped (rhombohedral) crystals, often with curved faces; also massive or granular

CLEAVAGE:
Perfect (rhombohedral)

HARDNESS:
3.5–4

SG:
4

LUSTER:
Crystals vitreous to pearly; massive dull

TRANSPARENCY:
Translucent to opaque

TESTS:
Conchoidal to uneven fracture; brittle. Curved faces of crystals. Dissolves slowly in dilute HCl

LOOKALIKES:
Dolomite is paler

FAMILY: CALCIUM CARBONATE

ID FACT FILE

CRYSTAL SYSTEM:
Orthorhombic

COLOR:
White, yellowish, or gray

WHERE:
Sedimentary, hydrothermal

ABUNDANCE:
Abundant

FORM:
Sharp pointed prismatic crystals, often twinned; radiating acicular needles, also corals, stalactites, and encrusting forms

CLEAVAGE:
Perfect (rhombohedral)

HARDNESS:
3.5–4

SG:
2.9

LUSTER:
Vitreous

TRANSPARENCY:
Transparent to translucent

TESTS:
Subconchoidal fracture; brittle. Dissolves easily in dilute HCl

LOOKALIKES:
Calcite is less hard

Aragonite • $CaCO_3$

Chemical group: Carbonate

Aragonite is the high-pressure form (polymorph) of $CaCO_3$ calcite, into which it changes upon heating. Small amounts of lead and strontium may be present. It can occur with sedimentary gypsum deposits, and is also accreted biologically to form the basic structure of many corals. It is slightly harder than calcite where it occurs as prismatic crystals (*see* photograph); these are of a different shape to calcite.

FAMILY: COPPER CARBONATE

Azurite •
$Cu_3(CO_3)_2(OH)_2$

Chemical group: Carbonate

ID FACT FILE

CRYSTAL SYSTEM:
Monoclinic

COLOR:
Deep blue (azure blue)

WHERE:
Hydrothermal

ABUNDANCE:
Common

FORM:
Prismatic crystals uncommon, sometimes radiating aggregates, often massive

CLEAVAGE:
Good

HARDNESS:
3.5–4

SG:
3.8

LUSTER:
Vitreous

TRANSPARENCY:
Transparent to opaque

TESTS:
Conchoidal fracture; brittle. Effervesces in dilute HCl. Pale blue streak

LOOKALIKES:
Unlikely to confuse color and streak

Azurite is a basic hydrated copper carbonate, similar to malachite. It has a distinctive deep azure blue color and has been used as a pigment. It occurs as a secondary copper mineral in the oxidized zone of hydrothermal veins and porphyry copper deposits, often together with malachite, cuprite, and native copper, as in San Juan, Utah. The photograph shows rare substantial crystals of azurite.

FAMILY: CALCIUM CARBONATE

ID FACT FILE

CRYSTAL SYSTEM:
Hexagonal-trigonal

COLOR:
Colorless, white; sometimes tinted with other colors

WHERE:
Igneous, sedimentary, metamorphic

ABUNDANCE:
Rock-forming

FORM:
Prismatic crystals of several varieties, commonly twinned; also occurs nodular, granular, stalactitic, compact, earthy

CLEAVAGE:
Perfect (rhombohedral)

HARDNESS:
3

SG:
2.71

LUSTER:
Vitreous to earthy

TRANSPARENCY:
Transparent to opaque

TESTS:
Conchoidal but cleaves easily. Dissolves in dilute HCl. White streak

LOOKALIKES:
Carbonates

Calcite • $CaCO_3$

Chemical group: Carbonate

Calcite is the principal rock-forming mineral of several sedimentary rocks, including limestones and chalk. It forms the shells of many biological organisms. It also occurs as a hydrothermal mineral, as a primary mineral in igneous carbonatite, and is widespread in metamorphic rocks. Calcite may be of organic or inorganic origin. It may contain a variety of impurities including iron, magnesium, manganese, lead, and strontium. "Dogtooth spar" (illustrated) and "Iceland spar" are particularly well formed crystal varieties of calcite.

FAMILY: LEAD CARBONATE

ID FACT FILE

CRYSTAL SYSTEM:
Orthorhombic

COLOR:
Colorless, white or grayish; sometimes tinted blue or green

WHERE:
Hydrothermal

ABUNDANCE:
Restricted

FORM:
Prismatic tabular crystals; twinning can give cruciform or radiating aggregates; also stalactitic, massive

CLEAVAGE:
Imperfect

HARDNESS:
3–3.5

SG:
6.6

LUSTER:
Adamantine, vitreous, or resinous

TRANSPARENCY:
Transparent to opaque

TESTS:
Conchoidal, brittle. Dissolves in dilute HCl. White streak

LOOKALIKES:
Barite

Cerussite • $PbCO_3$

Chemical group: Carbonate

Cerussite is simple lead carbonate. It occurs in the weathering zone of lead deposits, and is often associated with galena and anglesite. It occurs at most lead mineral localities and is locally an important lead ore. As for many carbonate minerals it dissolves in dilute hydrochloric acid (HCl). High density (SG) can be distinctive.

FAMILY: COMPOUND CARBONATE

ID FACT FILE

CRYSTAL SYSTEM:
Hexagonal-trigonal

COLOR:
Colorless, white, pink, grayish, or various tints

WHERE:
Igneous, sedimentary, metamorphic

ABUNDANCE:
Rock-forming

FORM:
Prismatic crystals, frequently curved, mostly rhombohedral; also massive, porous or granular

CLEAVAGE:
Perfect

HARDNESS:
3.5–4

SG:
2.9

LUSTER:
Vitreous

TRANSPARENCY:
Transparent to translucent

TESTS:
Conchoidal fracture, brittle. Dissolves slowly in dilute HCl. White or pale gray streak

LOOKALIKES:
Ankerite

Dolomite • $CaMg(CO_3)_2$

Chemical group: Carbonate

Dolomite is a mixed calcium-magnesium carbonate. It is a rock-forming mineral in sedimentary dolomites, metamorphic marbles, and together with calcite in limestones. It also occurs in hydrothermal mineral veins. Dolomite forms a complete compositional series with ankerite. In addition to iron, impurities may include manganese, strontium, and lead. Crystalline forms can have distinctive curved crystal edges. Dissolves reluctantly in dilute HCl.

FAMILY: MAGNESIUM CARBONATE

ID FACT FILE

CRYSTAL SYSTEM:
Hexagonal-trigonal

COLOR:
White, grayish, or brownish; chalky

WHERE:
Hydrothermal

ABUNDANCE:
Restricted

FORM:
Usually massive, fibrous, or granular; rare crystals similar to dolomite

CLEAVAGE:
Perfect

HARDNESS:
3.5–4.5

SG:
3

LUSTER:
Fibrous earthy; crystals vitreous

TRANSPARENCY:
Transparent to opaque

TESTS:
Flat conchoidal fracture. Dissolves slowly in dilute HCl. White streak

LOOKALIKES:
Chalk

Magnesite • $MgCO_3$

Chemical group: Carbonate

Magnesite is a simple magnesium carbonate. It occurs as a secondary replacement vein mineral in ultramafic rocks altered by fluids; sometimes it also forms significant bodies of magnesite-rich rock by metasomatic replacement of original sedimentary dolomite and limestone adjacent to intrusive igneous rocks. Crystalline forms are rare and in its normal massive white form it closely resembles the rock chalk, but is somewhat harder than calcite.

FAMILY: COPPER CARBONATE

ID FACT FILE

CRYSTAL SYSTEM:
Monoclinic

COLOR:
Bright green, often banded

WHERE:
Hydrothermal

ABUNDANCE:
Common

FORM:
Usually massive, encrusting, stalactitic with smooth botryoidal surface; internally fibrous, compact, or earthy

CLEAVAGE:
Perfect

HARDNESS:
3.5–4

SG:
3.9

LUSTER:
Silky to earthy

TRANSPARENCY:
Translucent (crystals) to opaque

TESTS:
Flat conchoidal fracture. Green streak

LOOKALIKES:
Chrysocolla

Malachite •
$Cu_2CO_3(OH)_2$

Chemical group: Carbonate

The attractive green colors of malachite are distinctive, and it is often polished as an ornament. It is perhaps the best-known copper carbonate mineral. Its bright green colors have been used as a pigment. The color banding represents successive growth from hydrothermal fluids, in veins and in the oxidized zone of copper deposits. It often occurs with azurite, as in Zambia, in Africa; San Juan, Utah; and other secondary copper minerals.

FAMILY: MANGANESE CARBONATE

ID FACT FILE

CRYSTAL SYSTEM:
Hexagonal-trigonal

COLOR:
Raspberry or rose-red to brown

WHERE:
Hydrothermal

ABUNDANCE:
Common

FORM:
Usually massive, globular, botryoidal; rare crystals often curved

CLEAVAGE:
Perfect

HARDNESS:
3.5–4.5

SG:
3.4–3.6

LUSTER:
Vitreous to pearly

TRANSPARENCY:
Translucent

TESTS:
Uneven, brittle. White streak

LOOKALIKES:
Dolomite

Rhodochrosite • $MnCO_3$

Chemical group: Carbonate

Rhodochrosite is a simple manganese carbonate and a relative of siderite. It occurs in hydrothermal vein systems and stockworks, often associated with lead and silver-lead minerals; it also occurs as a metasomatic replacement in sedimentary rocks. Massive forms often show wavy concentric successive growth layers and distinctive pink colors.

FAMILY: MANGANESE CARBONATE

ID FACT FILE

CRYSTAL SYSTEM:
Hexagonal-trigonal

COLOR:
Yellowish, brown

WHERE:
Sedimentary, hydrothermal

ABUNDANCE:
Common

FORM:
Tabular crystals often slightly curved; also massive, granular, or oolitic

CLEAVAGE:
Perfect

HARDNESS:
4–4.5

SG:
3.7–3.9

LUSTER:
Vitreous to pearly

TRANSPARENCY:
Translucent

TESTS:
Conchoidal, brittle. White, or brownish streak

LOOKALIKES:
Dolomite, ankerite

Siderite • FeCO$_3$

Chemical group: Carbonate

Siderite, iron carbonate, occurs in hydrothermal vein systems and stockworks, as for rhodochrosite. It occurs most widely in sedimentary rocks; it forms the ooliths in oolitic ironstone, and beds and nodules in clay ironstone especially of Carboniferous age. It also occurs as a metasomatic replacement in sedimentary rocks and can be an important ore mineral of iron. An important rock-forming mineral in some ironstone (*see* p.224). Photograph shows cluster of tabular crystals.

ID FACT FILE

CRYSTAL SYSTEM:
Orthorhombic

COLOR:
Gray, white,
slightly tinted

WHERE:
Hydrothermal,
sedimentary,
igneous

ABUNDANCE:
Restricted

FORM:
Prismatic,
acicular, spiky or
fibrous crystals;
often twinned
like aragonite

CLEAVAGE:
Imperfect

HARDNESS:
3.5

SG:
3.7

LUSTER:
Vitreous to
resinous

TRANSPARENCY:
Transparent to
opaque

TESTS:
Conchoidal,
brittle. White
streak

LOOKALIKES:
Aragonite is
lower density

Strontianite • $SrCO_3$

Chemical group: Carbonate

Strontianite occurs in hydrothermal vein
systems sometimes associated with fluorite,
galena, and barite, as at type locality in
Strontian, in Scotland, and Weardale, in
England. It also occurs as nodules and as a
replacement mineral in sedimentary carbonate
rocks including Cretaceous marls and
limestones in Germany. Rarely it is seen as a
primary mineral in igneous carbonatites. It has
higher SG than many other carbonates.

FAMILY: BARIUM CARBONATE

ID FACT FILE

CRYSTAL SYSTEM:
Orthorhombic

COLOR:
White with tints
of gray, yellow, or
pink

WHERE:
Hydrothermal

ABUNDANCE:
Restricted

FORM:
Columnar
crystals often
twinned and
pointed
pseudohexagonal
shapes; also
massive

CLEAVAGE:
Poor

HARDNESS:
3–3.5

SG:
4.3

LUSTER:
Vitreous to
resinous

TRANSPARENCY:
Transparent to
translucent

TESTS:
Uneven, brittle.
White streak

LOOKALIKES:
Barite

Witherite • BaCO$_3$

Chemical group: Carbonate

Witherite occurs in hydrothermal vein systems
sometimes as the matrix; often associated with
galena and barite as in Alston Moor, in
England and Hardin County, Illinois. Easily
mistaken for barite when good crystal forms
are absent. It has higher SG than most other
carbonate minerals, including strontianite.
Photograph shows pseudohexagonal crystals.

FAMILY: LEAD SULFATE

ID FACT FILE

CRYSTAL SYSTEM:
Orthorhombic

COLOR:
White with tints of gray, blue, or yellow

WHERE:
Hydrothermal

ABUNDANCE:
Restricted

FORM:
Tabular, prismatic crystals; also granular or stalactitic

CLEAVAGE:
Imperfect

HARDNESS:
3–3.5

SG:
6.3–6.4

LUSTER:
Adamantine, greasy

TRANSPARENCY:
Transparent to opaque

TESTS:
Conchoidal fracture, brittle. White streak

LOOKALIKES:
Barite

Anglesite • PbSO$_4$

Chemical group: Sulfate

Anglesite, lead sulfate, occurs commonly in the oxidation zone of hydrothermal systems containing galena in association with other carbonate minerals, as in Angleey, in Wales; also Cornwall and Cumberland, in England, Austria, and Spain. It usually forms small crystals and if sufficient in quantity has distinctive high density. Crystal faces often striated and often much smaller than barite, with which it may occur.

FAMILY: CALCIUM SULFATE

ID FACT FILE

CRYSTAL SYSTEM:
Orthorhombic

COLOR:
White with tints
of gray, blue, or
yellow

WHERE:
Sedimentary

ABUNDANCE:
Rock-forming

FORM:
Tabular,
prismatic
crystals; also
fibrous, massive
or granular

CLEAVAGE:
Perfect giving
rectangular
fragments

HARDNESS:
3–3.5

SG:
2.9–3

LUSTER:
Pearly

TRANSPARENCY:
Transparent to
translucent

TESTS:
Conchoidal
fracture, brittle.
White streak

LOOKALIKES:
Halite is softer

Anhydrite • CaSO$_4$

Chemical group: Sulfate

Anhydrite changes slowly to gypsum through
the addition of water. It is widespread and
occurs in salt deposits where, associated with
gypsum, it often makes the impermeable cap
rock. It may form alternating sedimentary
layers with gypsum in evaporite deposits.
Fibrous form (shown) easily distinguished
from gypsum by greater hardness).

FAMILY: BARIUM SULFATE

ID FACT FILE

CRYSTAL SYSTEM:
Orthorhombic

COLOR:
Colorless, white with tints of yellow or pink; occasionally bluish

WHERE:
Hydrothermal, sedimentary

ABUNDANCE:
Common

FORM:
Tabular crystals often prominent terminations; also massive

CLEAVAGE:
Perfect parallel to length

HARDNESS:
3–3.5

SG:
4.5

LUSTER:
Vitreous, pearly

TRANSPARENCY:
Transparent to translucent

TESTS:
Uneven, brittle. White streak

LOOKALIKES:
Witherite in massive form, celestine

Barite • BaSO$_4$

Chemical group: Sulfate

Barite, a common barium sulfate, is common as a secondary mineral in limestones, and as concretions and occasionally cement of sandstones as in Derbyshire, in England and in Elgin, in Scotland. It often contains calcium and strontium impurities and occurs commonly in hydrothermal vein deposits with lead and zinc minerals. It occurs in some igneous carbonatites. Where crystals are absent, the massive white form has distinctly high SG.

FAMILY: STRONTIUM SULFATE

ID FACT FILE

CRYSTAL SYSTEM:
Orthorhombic

COLOR:
White tinted pale
blue or yellow

WHERE:
Sedimentary,
hydrothermal

ABUNDANCE:
Rock-forming

FORM:
Tabular,
prismatic
crystals; also
fibrous, massive,
or granular

CLEAVAGE:
Perfect

HARDNESS:
3–3.5

SG:
3.9–4.0

LUSTER:
Vitreous, pearly

TRANSPARENCY:
Transparent to
translucent

TESTS:
Conchoidal
fracture, brittle.
White streak

LOOKALIKES:
Barite

Celestine • $SrSO_4$

Chemical group: Sulfate

Celestite, strontium sulfate, occurs as
sedimentary beds associated with gypsum and
halite in evaporite deposits. The beds are
typically nodular and uneven; celestite also
forms concretions in limestone. It occasionally
occurs in cavities in volcanic rocks, and is
associated with sulfur deposits in Sicily, in Italy.
Also occurs as an accessory mineral in some
varieties of igneous carbonatite and pegmatite.

FAMILY: HYDRATED CALCIUM SULFATE

Gypsum • $CaSO_4 \cdot 2H_2O$

Chemical group: Sulfate

ID FACT FILE

CRYSTAL SYSTEM:
Monoclinic

COLOR:
Colorless, white, gray, yellowish, or red

WHERE:
Sedimentary

ABUNDANCE:
Rock-forming

FORM:
Prismatic twinned crystals common; also fibrous, massive, or granular

CLEAVAGE:
Perfect

HARDNESS:
1.5–2.0

SG:
2.3

LUSTER:
Vitreous, pearly

TRANSPARENCY:
Transparent to opaque

TESTS:
Conchoidal fracture, brittle. White streak

LOOKALIKES:
Crystals unlikely to be mistaken

Gypsum occurs throughout the world in salt and evaporite deposits, and also as a secondary mineral in some clays and dolomitized limestones; impurities cause the variation in colors. Alabaster is a snow-white compact variety. Desert rose is an aggregate of sand grains cemented by gypsum into a rosette. Low hardness means it can be scratched by a fingernail. Twinned crystals (as illustrated) are common.

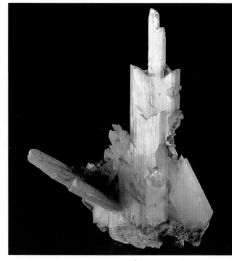

ID FACT FILE

CRYSTAL SYSTEM:
Hexagonal

COLOR:
Often pale green, bluish, or yellow; all colors

WHERE:
Igneous, metamorphic, sedimentary

ABUNDANCE:
Abundant

FORM:
Columnar or well shaped elongated prisms; also massive, granular, and radiating

CLEAVAGE:
Imperfect

HARDNESS:
5

SG:
3.16–3.22

LUSTER:
Greasy, vitreous

TRANSPARENCY:
Transparent to opaque

TESTS:
Conchoidal, uneven, brittle fracture. White streak

LOOKALIKES:
Quartz

Apatite • $Ca_5(PO_4)_3F$

Chemical group: Phosphate

Apatite, or fluorapatite, occurs in small amounts in most igneous and metamorphic rocks. It also occurs in sedimentary rocks such as concretions in limestones. It can be a rock-forming mineral in marine-bedded deposits. Chlorine can replace fluorine, and other impurities can include sodium and rare earth elements. Distinguished from quartz by lack of pointed crystal terminations and lower hardness.

FAMILY: LAZULITE

Lazulite •
$(Mg,Fe)Al_2(PO_4)_2(OH)_2$

Chemical group: Phosphate

ID FACT FILE

CRYSTAL SYSTEM:
Monoclinic

COLOR:
Blue

WHERE:
Igneous

ABUNDANCE:
Uncommon

FORM:
Elongated
crystals

CLEAVAGE:
Poor

HARDNESS:
5.5–6

SG:
3.1–3.2

LUSTER:
Vitreous,
adamantine

TRANSPARENCY:
Transparent to
opaque

TESTS:
Conchoidal,
uneven, brittle
fracture. White
streak

LOOKALIKES:
Azurite

Lazulite is an uncommon but distinctively blue-colored magnesium-rich phosphate. It occurs in igneous rocks, in pegmatites. Some forms resemble spherulitic or radiating zeolites in appearance. Impurities can include calcium. Photograph shows an enlargement of a small crystal.

FAMILY: MONAZITE

ID FACT FILE

CRYSTAL SYSTEM:
Monoclinic

COLOR:
White to dark brown or green

WHERE:
Igneous, metamorphic, sedimentary

ABUNDANCE:
Common

FORM:
Thick tabular crystals; also massive

CLEAVAGE:
Perfect

HARDNESS:
5–5.5

SG:
4.6–5.7

LUSTER:
Resinous

TRANSPARENCY:
Translucent to opaque

TESTS:
Conchoidal, brittle fracture. White streak. Radioactive

LOOKALIKES:
Apatite, orthoclase

Monazite • $(Ce,La)PO_4$

Chemical group: Phosphate

Monazite is a rare earth element (Ce,La) phosphate. It occurs as a minor constituent of quartz-rich igneous rocks such as granites, in some altered carbonatites and in pegmatites. It also occurs in some metamorphic rocks like gneiss; also in sedimentary placer deposits, as in Brazil. It usually contains a small percentage of thorium, making it mildly radioactive and a valuable source for this element, in addition to rare earth elements.

FAMILY: APATITE

Pyromorphite •
$Pb_5(PO_4)_3Cl$

Chemical group: Phosphate

ID FACT FILE

CRYSTAL SYSTEM:
Hexagonal

COLOR:
Green, brown, yellow; often vivid colors

WHERE:
Igneous

ABUNDANCE:
Restricted

FORM:
Prismatic, barrel- or needle-shaped crystals; also massive

CLEAVAGE:
None

HARDNESS:
3.5–4

SG:
6.7–7.1

LUSTER:
Adamantine, greasy

TRANSPARENCY:
Transparent to translucent

TESTS:
Conchoidal, uneven, brittle fracture. White streak

LOOKALIKES:
Apatite

Pyromorphite is a chlorophosphate which occurs as a secondary mineral in the oxidation zone of hydrothermal lead deposits, as in Cornwall, in England, and in Freiberg, Saxony, and Harz in Germany. Impurities include small amounts of calcium or arsenic. Associated often with other lead minerals including vanadinite, anglesite, and cerussite. High SG and bright colors can help identification.

FAMILY: VIVIANITE

Vivianite •
$Fe_3(PO_4)_2.8H_2O$

Chemical group: Phosphate

Vivianite is a hydrous iron phosphate. It occurs in vein systems as a secondary mineral associated with iron, tin, and copper deposits, as in St. Agnes, in Cornwall and Chihuahua, in Mexico. It also occurs in fossil bones and teeth, in clay-rich rocks, in bogs, as in Scotland, and in brown-coal deposits as in Germany. It is easily distinguished from other lookalikes by its translucent appearance and its notably low hardness—it is easily scratched with a fingernail.

ID FACT FILE

CRYSTAL SYSTEM:
Monoclinic

COLOR:
Colorless, white, blue, or green

WHERE:
Igneous, sedimentary

ABUNDANCE:
Common

FORM:
Crystals tabular or needlelike; granular, or earthy

CLEAVAGE:
Perfect

HARDNESS:
1.5–2

SG:
2.6–2.7

LUSTER:
Vitreous, metallic

TRANSPARENCY:
Translucent

TESTS:
Fibrous brittle, thin flexible. White changing to blue streak

LOOKALIKES:
Covellite, azurite

FAMILY: AMPHIBOLE

Actinolite • $Ca_2Fe_5Si_8O_{22}(OH)_2$

Chemical group: Silicate

ID FACT FILE

CRYSTAL SYSTEM:
Monoclinic

COLOR:
Green

WHERE:
Metamorphic

ABUNDANCE:
Common, rock-forming

FORM:
Slender bladed prisms or fibrous radiating bunches

CLEAVAGE:
Obvious parallel to length; two sets intersect at 120° on basal sections

HARDNESS:
5–6

SG:
2.9–3.2

LUSTER:
Vitreous

TRANSPARENCY:
Opaque

TESTS:
White streak; splintery fracture

LOOKALIKES:
Hornblende

Actinolite is the iron-rich relative of tremolite amphibole and occurs as a common mineral in a wide variety of metamorphic rocks, including schists and greenschists; it often replaces pyroxene and hornblende in metamorphosed igneous rocks. The intersection of two cleavages at 120° on basal sections is distinctive of amphiboles. *Nephrite* is a tougher massive variety similar to jadeite.

FAMILY: AMPHIBOLE

Glaucophane • $Na_2(Mg, Fe)_3Al_2Si_8O_{22}(OH)_2$

Chemical group: Silicate

ID FACT FILE

Crystal system:
Monoclinic

Color:
Blue or bluish gray

Where:
Metamorphic

Abundance:
Rare, rock-forming

Form:
Bladed prisms, fibrous, massive or granular

Cleavage:
Obvious parallel to length; two sets intersect at 120° on basal sections

Hardness:
6–6.5

SG:
3–3.1

Luster:
Vitreous

Transparency:
Translucent

Tests:
Grayish streak

Lookalikes:
Riebeckite

Glaucophane is a sodium-rich amphibole, with more magnesium than iron. It is a distinct blue and is a rock-forming mineral in rare high-pressure metamorphic areas where it forms blueschists, as in southern Brittany, in France, Anglesey, in Wales and Lac Malartic, in Quebec. Distinguished from blue riebeckite by the host rock type (riebeckite occurs in igneous rocks) and its greater hardness.

FAMILY: AMPHIBOLE

Hornblende • $(Ca,Mg,Fe, Na,Al)_7(Al,Si)_8O_{22}(OH)_2$

Chemical group: Silicate

ID FACT FILE

CRYSTAL SYSTEM:
Monoclinic

COLOR:
Black with tints of brown or green

WHERE:
Igneous, metamorphic

ABUNDANCE:
Abundant

FORM:
Chunky prisms or long bladed crystals

CLEAVAGE:
Obvious parallel to length; two sets intersect at 120° on basal sections

HARDNESS:
5–6

SG:
3–3.47

LUSTER:
Vitreous

TRANSPARENCY:
Opaque to translucent

TESTS:
Crystals often twinned in volcanic rocks. Uneven fracture

LOOKALIKES:
Augite; where twinned, hornblende has no re-entrant angle

Hornblende (see tall crystal below) is the commonest amphibole and occurs as a primary mineral in a wide variety of igneous rocks, often as well formed crystals in volcanic rocks. It is also very common in regional metamorphic rocks derived from igneous rocks. The intersection of two cleavages at ~120° on basal sections is distinctive of amphiboles; also cross sections of prismatic crystals are often six-sided whereas augite is eight-sided.

FAMILY: AMPHIBOLE

Riebeckite •
$Na_2Fe_5Si_8O_{22}(OH)_2$

Chemical group: Silicate

ID FACT FILE

CRYSTAL SYSTEM:
Monoclinic

COLOR:
Black, or dark blue

WHERE:
Igneous

ABUNDANCE:
Restricted

FORM:
Bladed prisms or fibrous radiating bunches

CLEAVAGE:
Obvious parallel to length; two sets intersect at 120° on basal sections

HARDNESS:
4

SG:
3.43

LUSTER:
Vitreous

TRANSPARENCY:
Opaque

TESTS:
Uneven fracture, brittle, blue-gray streak

LOOKALIKES:
Hornblende is harder

Riebeckite is an alkali-amphibole rich in sodium and iron. Its occurrence is restricted to silica-rich igneous rocks such as riebeckite granite, and riebeckite granophyre. It is the main dark rock-forming mineral in some small Scottish granites favored for use in the ice-sport of curling. A finely fibrous pale grayish blue variety called crocidolite has separable fibers and resembles chrysotile; it is also known as blue asbestos, and is hazardous.

FAMILY: AMPHIBOLE

Tremolite • $Ca_2Mg_5Si_8O_{22}(OH)_2$

Chemical group: Silicate

ID FACT FILE

CRYSTAL SYSTEM:
Monoclinic

COLOR:
White

WHERE:
Metamorphic

ABUNDANCE:
Common

FORM:
Slender bladed
prisms or fibrous
radiating
bunches

CLEAVAGE:
Obvious parallel
to length; two
sets intersect at
120° on basal
sections

HARDNESS:
5–6

SG:
2.9–3.2

LUSTER:
Vitreous

TRANSPARENCY:
Opaque

TESTS:
White color
distinguishes
from other
amphiboles

LOOKALIKES:
Hornblende and
other amphiboles

Tremolite is the magnesium-rich relative of actinolite amphibole and occurs as a common mineral in a wide variety of metamorphic rocks. It is particularly characteristic of metamorphosed calcareous rocks, derived from impure limestones, including marbles and calc-silicate hornfelses. The typical ~120° cleavage intersection of amphiboles can be almost impossible to observe in small fibrous forms, even with a hand lens. Photograph shows fibrous or asbestiform variety.

FAMILY: FELDSPAR

ID FACT FILE

CRYSTAL SYSTEM:
Triclinic

COLOR:
Colorless, white

WHERE:
Igneous,
metamorphic,
sedimentary

ABUNDANCE:
Rock-forming

FORM:
Tabular crystals,
often twinned;
also massive,
granular

CLEAVAGE:
Perfect

HARDNESS:
6–6.5

SG:
2.6–2.62

LUSTER:
Vitreous to pearly

TRANSPARENCY:
Transparent to
translucent

TESTS:
Uneven fracture.
White streak

LOOKALIKES:
Orthoclase,
microcline

Albite • $NaAlSi_3O_8$

Chemical group: Alumino-silicate

The feldspar group is the most abundant
mineral group in the Earth's crust, making up
more than 60 percent of the upper part. They
are all alumino-silicates with varying amounts
of the alkaline elements sodium, potassium,
and calcium. Albite is the pure sodium feldspar.
It may contain some calcium. It occurs in a
wide variety of igneous rocks including granite,
syenite, and pegmatites. It also occurs in
metamorphic schists and gneisses, and is a
common constituent of sedimentary arkose and
impure sandstones. The variety cleavelandite
occurs as platy white crystals in pegmatites.

FAMILY: PLAGIOCLASE FELDSPAR

ID FACT FILE

CRYSTAL SYSTEM:
Triclinic

COLOR:
Colorless or white

WHERE:
Igneous, metamorphic

ABUNDANCE:
Rock-forming

FORM:
Prismatic crystals, often massive

CLEAVAGE:
Perfect

HARDNESS:
6–6.5

SG:
2.74

LUSTER:
Vitreous to pearly

TRANSPARENCY:
Transparent to translucent

TESTS:
Conchoidal fracture. White streak

LOOKALIKES:
Albite, orthoclase

Anorthite • $CaAl_2Si_2O_8$

Chemical group: Alumino-silicate

Anorthite is the calcium-rich plagioclase usually with minor sodium and almost no potassium. It occurs in a few metamorphic hornfelses, but is typical of silica-poor igneous rocks like gabbro, troctolite, peridotite, and norite; it is almost the sole constituent of the igneous rock anorthosite, as in Rhum, in Scotland and Stillwater, Montana, and forming the bright, reflective highlands of the Moon. Photograph shows collection of igneous anorthite megacrysts.

FAMILY: FELDSPAR

ID FACT FILE

CRYSTAL SYSTEM:
Triclinic

COLOR:
White, pink,
yellow, gray

WHERE:
Igneous,
sedimentary

ABUNDANCE:
Abundant

FORM:
Tabular crystals,
often multiple
twinning; also
massive

CLEAVAGE:
Perfect

HARDNESS:
6

SG:
2.53–2.56

LUSTER:
Vitreous to pearly

TRANSPARENCY:
Transparent to
opaque

TESTS:
Conchoidal,
uneven, brittle
fracture. White
streak

LOOKALIKES:
Albite, orthoclase

Microcline • $KAlSi_3O_8$

Chemical group: Alumino-silicate

Microcline is distinguished from orthoclase by
fine parallel sets of striations on some faces
(basal) due to multiple sets of twinning;
otherwise physical properties are identical.
Microcline occurs in coarse-grained very
slowly cooled igneous rocks like granites and
pegmatites. A distinctive pale bluish-green
variety of microcline called *amazonite* is used
as a semiprecious gem material, as in Brazil.

FAMILY: FELDSPAR

ID FACT FILE

CRYSTAL SYSTEM:
Monoclinic

COLOR:
White, pink, yellow, gray

WHERE:
Igneous, metamorphic, sedimentary

ABUNDANCE:
Rock-forming

FORM:
Tabular crystals, often twinned

CLEAVAGE:
Perfect; two sets intersect at 90° on some faces

HARDNESS:
6

SG:
2.53–2.56

LUSTER:
Vitreous to pearly

TRANSPARENCY:
Transparent to opaque

TESTS:
Conchoidal, uneven, brittle fracture. White streak

LOOKALIKES:
Albite

Orthoclase • $KAlSi_3O_8$

Chemical group: Alumino-silicate

Orthoclase is the typical alkali feldspar with hardness of exactly 6. It is the dominant mineral in coarse-grained silica-rich igneous rocks like granite and syenite; it forms particularly large crystals in pegmatites. It sometimes contains impurities of barium. Common in many metamorphic rocks, it also occurs to a lesser extent in sedimentary rocks. The transparent variety *adularia* occurs in cavities in metamorphic rocks. Often distinguished from albite or plagioclase by pinkish color.

Plagioclase • $CaAl_2Si_2O_8$ to $NaAlSi_3O_8$

Chemical group: Alumino-silicate

ID FACT FILE

CRYSTAL SYSTEM:
Triclinic

COLOR:
Colorless, white, gray, greenish

WHERE:
Igneous, metamorphic, sedimentary

ABUNDANCE:
Rock-forming

FORM:
Prismatic, tabular crystals, multiply twinned

CLEAVAGE:
Perfect

HARDNESS:
6–6.5

SG:
2.61–2.77

LUSTER:
Vitreous to pearly

TRANSPARENCY:
Transparent to translucent

TESTS:
Conchoidal, uneven, brittle fracture. White streak

LOOKALIKES:
Orthoclase

Plagioclase feldspars show complete compositional variation between sodium plagioclase, albite, and calcium plagioclase, anorthite (*see* separate entries, p.89 and p.90). Crystal shapes are generally tabular or prismatic and feature multiple twins parallel to length; sometimes visible with a hand lens on cleaved surfaces. Plagioclase occurs widely, primarily in igneous and metamorphic rocks worldwide. Compositions with 30–50 percent albite (variety *labradorite*) often show an internal, oriented play of peacock colors (*schillerization*) dominated by blues and greens.

FAMILY: FELDSPAR

ID FACT FILE

CRYSTAL SYSTEM:
Monoclinic

COLOR:
Colorless, white, gray

WHERE:
Igneous

ABUNDANCE:
Rock-forming

FORM:
Tabular crystals

CLEAVAGE:
Perfect

HARDNESS:
6

SG:
2.53–2.56

LUSTER:
Vitreous to pearly

TRANSPARENCY:
Transparent to opaque

TESTS:
Conchoidal, uneven, brittle fracture. White streak. Simple twins

LOOKALIKES:
Albite, orthoclase

Sanidine • $KAlSi_3O_8$

Chemical group: Alumino-silicate

Sanidine is the high-temperature form of orthoclase and is similarly sodium-poor. It occurs as prominent glassy crystals in some volcanic lavas like trachyte and phonolite. The sodium-rich equivalent is called *anorthoclase*, which belongs to the triclinic crystal system; it forms colorless to white crystals of slightly different shape, including prominent rhombs, as in the Permian volcanics near Oslo, in Norway. Photograph shows twinned phenocrysts from volcanic rock.

FAMILY: FELDSPATHOID

Hauyne • $(Na,Ca)_{4-8}$ $Al_6Si_6(O,S)_{24}(SO_4,Cl)_{1-2}$

Chemical group: Aluminum silicate

ID FACT FILE

CRYSTAL SYSTEM:
Cubic

COLOR:
Blue, dark blue, greenish blue; powdery blue

WHERE:
Igneous

ABUNDANCE:
Restricted

FORM:
Small crystals with rounded or square outlines; aggregates

CLEAVAGE:
Good

HARDNESS:
5.5–6

SG:
2.4–2.5

LUSTER:
Vitreous, pearly

TRANSPARENCY:
Translucent to opaque

TESTS:
Conchoidal fracture. White streak

LOOKALIKES:
Sodalite

Hauyne usually forms aggregates of small crystals with a distinct blue color, generally less vivid than sodalite; on exposed rock surfaces it alters to a powdery whitish blue. Often occurs with similar composition mineral nosean. As for other feldspathoids (*see* nepheline, p.97) it occurs in igneous rocks that are low in silica and alkali-rich like phonolite, tephrite, and melilitite. Hauyne is relatively common in young alkaline volcanic rocks such as Vesuvius, in Naples, in Italy and in Eifel, in Germany.

FAMILY: FELDSPATHOID

Leucite • KAlSi$_2$O$_6$

Chemical group: Potassium aluminum silicate

ID FACT FILE

CRYSTAL SYSTEM:
Tetragonal; cubic above 600°C/1112°F

COLOR:
White, ash-gray

WHERE:
Igneous

ABUNDANCE:
Rock-forming

FORM:
Equant crystals with hexagonal or square outlines

CLEAVAGE:
None

HARDNESS:
5.5–6

SG:
2.45–2.5

LUSTER:
Dull, vitreous, pearly

TRANSPARENCY:
Translucent to opaque

TESTS:
Conchoidal, brittle fracture. White streak

LOOKALIKES:
Garnet

Leucite is a potassium-rich feldspathoid (*see* nepheline, p.97). It is a major constituent of potassium-rich silica-poor volcanic rocks like phonolite, tephrite, and leucite basalt. Its distinctive white crystals are particularly well known from many Italian volcanoes, including Vesuvius, Pompeii, Alban Hills, and Roccamonfina; locally known as "Vesuvian garnet." It is also found in southern Spain, in France, in Kaiserstuhl, in Baden, in Germany, and in the Bearpaw Mountains, Montana.

FAMILY: FELDSPATHOID

Nepheline •
(Na,K)AlSiO$_4$

Chemical group: Alumino-silicate

Feldspathoids are alumino-silicates like feldspars, but have larger amounts of alkaline elements and less silica.

Nepheline is probably the most abundant feldspathoid. It always contains some potassium and a small excess of silica compared with the ideal composition. It is a major constituent of many alkaline igneous rocks like nepheline syenite, and ijolite; it also occurs in alkaline volcanic rocks like nephelinite and phonolite, as in flood lavas in East Africa. It is prone to weathering and may develop crystal-shaped hollows on exposed rock surfaces.

ID FACT FILE

CRYSTAL SYSTEM:
Hexagonal

COLOR:
White, yellowish, colorless

WHERE:
Igneous

ABUNDANCE:
Rock-forming

FORM:
Short prismatic crystals with prominent six-sided or square outlines; also massive in pegmatites

CLEAVAGE:
Poor

HARDNESS:
5.5–6

SG:
2.6–2.65

LUSTER:
Vitreous, greasy

TRANSPARENCY:
Transparent to opaque

TESTS:
Conchoidal, uneven, brittle fracture. White streak

LOOKALIKES:
Quartz, melilite

FAMILY: FELDSPATHOID

Nosean •
$Na_8Al_6Si_6O_{24}(SO_4)$

Chemical group: Alumino-silicate

Nosean is similar in appearance to nepheline, with which it is often associated; it is also similar in composition, except that it contains sulfate. As for other feldspathoids (*see* nepheline, p.97) nosean occurs in igneous rocks that are low in silica and alkali-rich like syenite, phonolite, tephrite, and melilitite. Nosean is locally common in young alkaline volcanic rocks as in Naples, in Italy and Lake Laacher, in Eifel, in Germany.

ID FACT FILE

CRYSTAL SYSTEM:
Cubic

COLOR:
Gray, bluish, yellowish

WHERE:
Igneous

ABUNDANCE:
Restricted

FORM:
Crystals with squarish outlines; aggregates

CLEAVAGE:
Perfect

HARDNESS:
5.5

SG:
2.4–2.5

LUSTER:
Vitreous, greasy

TRANSPARENCY:
Transparent to opaque

TESTS:
Conchoidal fracture. White streak

LOOKALIKES:
Nepheline

FAMILY: FELDSPATHOID

Sodalite • $Na_4Al_3Si_3O_{12}Cl$

Chemical group: Sodium aluminum silicate

ID FACT FILE

CRYSTAL SYSTEM:
Cubic

COLOR:
Lavender-blue, grayish blue, white, yellowish

WHERE:
Igneous

ABUNDANCE:
Rock-forming

FORM:
Equant crystals; aggregates or massive

CLEAVAGE:
Good

HARDNESS:
5–6

SG:
2.1–2.3

LUSTER:
Vitreous, greasy

TRANSPARENCY:
Transparent to translucent

TESTS:
Uneven, conchoidal fracture. White streak

LOOKALIKES:
Hauyne

Sodalite is a chlorine-bearing feldspathoid that usually forms aggregates of small crystals, or massive areas with a distinctive clear blue color, more vivid than hauyne. Like other feldspathoids (*see* nepheline, p.97) it occurs in igneous rocks low in silica and alkali-rich, such as syenite, phonolite, tephrite, and melilitite. Sodalite can be a rock-forming mineral. Found also in alkaline volcanic rocks such as Vesuvius, in Naples, and the Aeolian Islands, both in Italy, and Eifel in Germany. Another blue mineral similar to sodalite, *lazurite*, is the chief constituent of the blue gem material *lapis lazuli*, found in Chile and Afghanistan.

FAMILY: GARNET

ID FACT FILE

CRYSTAL SYSTEM:
Cubic

COLOR:
Deep red

WHERE:
Metamorphic

ABUNDANCE:
Very common

FORM:
Euhedral equant cubic crystals often with good crystal faces (rhombododeca-hedron = 12 faces, trapezohedron = 24 faces)

CLEAVAGE:
None

HARDNESS:
6.5–7.5

SG:
3.9–4.2

LUSTER:
Vitreous

TRANSPARENCY:
Opaque to translucent or deep red transparent

TESTS:
Subconchoidal or uneven fracture. Relatively high density for silicate minerals

LOOKALIKES:
Garnets

Almandine •
$Fe_3Al_2(SiO_4)_3$
Chemical group: Silicate

Almandine is the commonest type of garnet occurring in metamorphic rocks such as mica-schists and garnet gneisses. Also referred to as "common garnet," which is brownish red, the translucent attractive deep red variety is semi-precious, and therefore sought after in recent detrital deposits where it is often rounded. The lack of cleavage, combined with high hardness and resistance to weathering, means garnet is often present as a "heavy mineral" in sediments. A brown relative particularly rich in manganese called "spessartine" is uncommon.

ID FACT FILE

Crystal system:
Cubic

Color:
Dark brown, greenish or yellowish brown

Where:
Metamorphic

Abundance:
Common

Form:
Euhedral equant cubic crystals often with good crystal faces called rhombododeca-hedron (12 faces) or trapezohedron (24 faces)

Cleavage:
None

Hardness:
7.0 or greater

SG:
3.8

Luster:
Vitreous

Transparency:
Opaque

Tests:
Subconchoidal or uneven fracture. Relatively high density for silicate minerals

Lookalikes:
Garnets

FAMILY: GARNET

Andradite •
$Ca_3Fe_2(SiO_4)_3$

Chemical group: Silicate

Andradite is the calcium-rich and generally less attractive relative of common garnet (almandine) except for a bright green gem variety called *demantoid* (illustrated). It occurs generally in metamorphic rocks, though a black variety called "melanite" occurs in alkaline igneous rocks such as nepheline syenites. As for all garnets, distinctive features in well crystalline forms may include characteristic garnet shape (*see* Form) and absence of cleavage and twinning. Photograph shows natural and cut gem forms.

FAMILY: GARNET

ID FACT FILE

CRYSTAL SYSTEM:
Cubic

COLOR:
Pale green, greenish white

WHERE:
Metamorphic

ABUNDANCE:
Restricted

FORM:
Euhedral equant cubic crystals often with good crystal faces (rhombododeca-hedron = 12 faces)

CLEAVAGE:
None

HARDNESS:
Just harder than quartz (i.e. 7)

SG:
3.5

LUSTER:
Vitreous

TRANSPARENCY:
Opaque to translucent

TESTS:
Conchoidal or uneven fracture (soluble in hydrochloric acid)

LOOKALIKES:
Garnets

Grossular • $Ca_3Al_2(SiO_4)_3$

Chemical group: Silicate

Grossular is a calcium-rich garnet characteristic of metamorphosed impure limestones or marble. Semiprecious transparent varieties with yellowish or pinkish color occasionally occur. It can occur at the contact between igneous rocks and older rocks in *skarn*. Photograph shows natural and cut gem forms.

FAMILY: GARNET

ID FACT FILE

CRYSTAL SYSTEM:
Cubic

COLOR:
Deep crimson-red with violet tints

WHERE:
Metamorphic

ABUNDANCE:
Restricted

FORM:
Euhedral equant cubic crystals often rounded

CLEAVAGE:
None

HARDNESS:
7.5

SG:
3.7

LUSTER:
Vitreous

TRANSPARENCY:
Translucent to transparent

TESTS:
Conchoidal

LOOKALIKES:
Garnets

Pyrope • $Mg_3Al_2(SiO_4)_3$

Chemical group: Silicate

Pyrope is the magnesium-rich red garnet found in metamorphosed ultrabasic igneous rocks and is stable to very high pressures. It is characteristic of olivine-rich rocks like peridotite and lherzolite. It is present in the deepest samples of the Earth's upper mantle. Photograph shows group of partly rounded large crystals and a cut gem.

FAMILY: MICA

ID FACT FILE

CRYSTAL SYSTEM:
Monoclinic

COLOR:
Black, dark brown

WHERE:
Metamorphic, igneous

ABUNDANCE:
Rock-forming

FORM:
Hexagonal-shaped crystals; aggregates

CLEAVAGE:
Perfect

HARDNESS:
2.5–3

SG:
2.7–3.3

LUSTER:
Vitreous, pearly, metallic

TRANSPARENCY:
Transparent to opaque

TESTS:
Platy fracture, flexible. White streak

LOOKALIKES:
Phlogopite, chlorite

Biotite • $K(Mg,Fe)_3$ $(Al,Fe)Si_3O_{10}(OH,F)_2$

Chemical group: Hydrous silicate

Biotite is an important constituent of many igneous rocks, like granite, diorite, and andesite. It is also a rock-forming mineral in metamorphic rocks like gneiss, schist, and hornfels. It contains variable amounts of magnesium and iron and may contain small amounts of titanium. It often weathers to a pale golden color, when it resembles phlogopite (see p.107).

FAMILY: MICA

Lepidolite • $K(Li,Al)_3$ $(Si,Al)_4O_{10}(F,OH)_2$

Chemical group: Hydrous silicate

ID FACT FILE

CRYSTAL SYSTEM:
Monoclinic

COLOR:
Violet, rose-pink

WHERE:
Igneous

ABUNDANCE:
Restricted

FORM:
Hexagonal-shaped crystals; platy aggregates

CLEAVAGE:
Perfect

HARDNESS:
2–3

SG:
2.8–2.9

LUSTER:
Pearly, vitreous

TRANSPARENCY:
Transparent to translucent

TESTS:
Platy fracture, elastic, flexible. White streak

LOOKALIKES:
Unlikely to be mistaken

Lepidolite is a lithium-rich mica, usually with very distinctive violet to pink color. It occurs in silica-rich igneous rocks like granite and pegmatite, and is often associated with other lithium-bearing minerals like tourmaline, as in Cornwall, in England, California, and Minas Gerias, in Brazil. Like all micas, it has perfect cleavage, and individual flakes can be separated with a fingernail.

FAMILY: MICA

Muscovite •
$KAl_2(Si_3Al)O_{10}(OH)_2$

Chemical group: Hydrous silicate

ID FACT FILE

CRYSTAL SYSTEM:
Monoclinic

COLOR:
Colorless, lightly tinted

WHERE:
Metamorphic, igneous, sedimentary

ABUNDANCE:
Rock-forming

FORM:
Hexagonal-shaped crystals; platy aggregates

CLEAVAGE:
Perfect

HARDNESS:
2–3

SG:
2.8–2.9

LUSTER:
Pearly, metallic

TRANSPARENCY:
Transparent to translucent

TESTS:
Platy fracture, flexible. White streak

LOOKALIKES:
Phlogopite

Like all micas, muscovite reflects light strongly from broken platy fragments (cleavage flakes) and glistens. It occurs as an essential constituent of silica-rich igneous rocks like granite, greisen, and pegmatite. It occurs widely in metamorphic rocks like gneiss and mica-schist. It is a common mineral resistant to weathering and occurs in sedimentary rocks like micaceous sandstone. *Sericite* is a claylike variety formed by alteration of feldspars. Muscovite concentrations are found in Russia, India, the United States, and Canada.

FAMILY: MICA

Phlogopite •
$KMg_3AlSi_3O_{10}(F,OH)_2$

Chemical group: Hydrous silicate

ID FACT FILE

CRYSTAL SYSTEM:
Monoclinic

COLOR:
Pale brown, reddish brown, gray

WHERE:
Metamorphic, igneous

ABUNDANCE:
Rock-forming

FORM:
Hexagonal-shaped crystals; aggregates

CLEAVAGE:
Perfect

HARDNESS:
2.5–3

SG:
2.7–2.9

LUSTER:
Pearly, metallic

TRANSPARENCY:
Transparent to translucent

TESTS:
Platy fracture, flexible. White streak

LOOKALIKES:
Biotite, muscovite

Phlogopite is a magnesium-rich mica. It is a paler color than biotite and sometimes has a golden tint. It is a primary constituent of ultrabasic igneous rocks like kimberlite, carbonatite, and lamprophyre. It also occurs in metamorphic rocks like impure marble. It usually contains impurities of iron and some titanium. Found in Canada, in Baikal in Russia, Sweden, Finland, Scotland, and elsewhere.

FAMILY: OLIVINE

ID FACT FILE

CRYSTAL SYSTEM:
Orthorhombic

COLOR:
Green, olive-green, rarely other colors

WHERE:
Igneous, metamorphic

ABUNDANCE:
Rock-forming

FORM:
Stubby prismatic crystals, also granular aggregates

CLEAVAGE:
Poor

HARDNESS:
6.5–7

SG:
3.27–4.20

LUSTER:
Vitreous to greasy

TRANSPARENCY:
Transparent to translucent

TESTS:
Conchoidal, brittle fracture. White streak

LOOKALIKES:
Chrome diopside (p.111)

Olivine • $(Mg,Fe)_2SiO_4$

Chemical group: Silicate

Olivine shows a complete compositional variation between forsterite (iron-free) and fayalite (magnesium-free). Typical green olivine with mixed iron and magnesium is the main mineral forming peridotites. It occurs in igneous rocks with low silica such as gabbro, basalt, dolerite; it forms slender crystals in komatiite. *Forsterite* can occur in metamorphic marble. *Fayalite* is dark brown or black; it is uncommon but can occur in granite pegmatites. The pale green semiprecious gem variety *peridote* is transparent, as found in the state of Hawaii and in San Carlos, Arizona.

FAMILY: PYROXENE

ID FACT FILE

CRYSTAL SYSTEM:
Monoclinic

COLOR:
Dark green to brown

WHERE:
Igneous

ABUNDANCE:
Common

FORM:
Prismatic crystals, acicular or radiating bunches

CLEAVAGE:
Distinctive parallel along prisms

HARDNESS:
6–6.5

SG:
3.5

LUSTER:
Vitreous

TRANSPARENCY:
Opaque to translucent

TESTS:
Strongly colored and easily distinguished in thin sections

LOOKALIKES:
Augite

Aegirine • $NaFe\ Si_2O_6$

Chemical group: Silicate

Aegirine is a sodium ferric iron pyroxene that forms a compositional gradation into augite. It can form radiating clusters or "rosettes." Basal sections show 90° cleavage intersection of pyroxene. The intermediate pyroxene, *aegirine-augite*, is black, and occurs widely in alkaline volcanic and igneous rocks, such as phonolites. Aegirine is characteristic of late-stage alkaline pegmatites and strongly alkaline plutonic igneous rocks such as nepheline syenites as in Mt. St. Hilaire, Quebec, in Canada.

Augite • $(Ca,Mg,Fe,Al)_2$ $(Si,Al)_2O_6$

Chemical group: Silicate

ID FACT FILE

CRYSTAL SYSTEM:
Monoclinic

COLOR:
Black or greenish black

WHERE:
Igneous and metamorphic

ABUNDANCE:
Abundant

FORM:
Short prismatic or elongate bladed crystals; sometimes irregular-shaped

CLEAVAGE:
Distinctive parallel along the length of crystals

HARDNESS:
5–6

SG:
3.2–3.5

LUSTER:
Vitreous to resinous

TRANSPARENCY:
Opaque

TESTS:
Diagnostic pyroxene cleavage. May show simple twinning

LOOKALIKES:
Hornblende

Augite is the commonest pyroxene, occurring widely in igneous rocks. It forms stumpy prismatic crystals in volcanic rocks, and longer flat-bladed crystals in basic dykes and sills such as dolerites. It also occurs in high-grade metamorphic rocks such as pyroxene-granulites. Basal sections show 90° cleavage intersection of pyroxene. Single crystals distinguished from hornblende by re-entrant angle when twinned, as along top edge of right-hand crystal shown.

FAMILY: PYROXENE

ID FACT FILE

CRYSTAL SYSTEM:
Monoclinic

COLOR:
White, green, or dark green

WHERE:
Igneous and metamorphic

ABUNDANCE:
Common

FORM:
Prismatic crystals or equant grains

CLEAVAGE:
Distinctive parallel to length of prisms

HARDNESS:
5–6

SG:
3.2–3.4

LUSTER:
Vitreous to resinous

TRANSPARENCY:
Opaque to transparent

TESTS:
Diagnostic pyroxene cleavage. Green color of chrome-rich variety distinctive

LOOKALIKES:
Distinguished from sometimes coexisting olivine by cleavage

Diopside • CaMg Si$_2$O$_6$

Chemical group: Silicate

Diopside is the magnesium-rich relative of hedenbergite. It is a monoclinic pyroxene or clinopyroxene. It typically occurs in metamorphosed impure limestones and marbles, where its pale green color may be distinctive. It also occurs in ultrabasic, metamorphic rocks such as lherzolites and wherlites, where the chromium-rich variety, *chrome-diopside*, has a vibrant apple-green color. Photograph shows several crystals with basal 90° pyroxene cleavage.

FAMILY: PYROXENE

ID FACT FILE

CRYSTAL SYSTEM:
Orthorhombic

COLOR:
Brown, bronze, gray

WHERE:
Igneous and metamorphic

ABUNDANCE:
Abundant

FORM:
Short prismatic or elongate bladed crystals; sometimes irregular-shaped

CLEAVAGE:
Distinctive parallel along the length of crystals. Basal prismatic sections show 90° cleavage intersection of pyroxene

HARDNESS:
5.5

SG:
3.1–3.3

LUSTER:
Vitreous to pearly

TRANSPARENCY:
Translucent to opaque

TESTS:
Diagnostic pyroxene cleavage

LOOKALIKES:
Augite

Enstatite • $Mg_2Si_2O_6$

Chemical group: Silicate

Enstatite is an orthorhombic pyroxene or orthopyroxene. It occurs widely in ultrabasic, basic, and intermediate igneous rocks such as pyroxenites, gabbros, and norites. The iron-bearing variety, *bronzite*, has a pearly metallic luster resembling bronze, and is often characteristic of serpentinized ultrabasic rocks such as wherlites and peridotites. Enstatite is also an important mineral in many meteorites.

FAMILY: PYROXENE

Hedenbergite • $CaFeSi_2O_6$

Chemical group: Silicate

ID FACT FILE

CRYSTAL SYSTEM:
Monoclinic

COLOR:
Black

WHERE:
Metamorphic or igneous

ABUNDANCE:
Uncommon

FORM:
Prismatic or bladed crystals

CLEAVAGE:
Obvious parallel along the length of crystals; basal sections show 90° cleavage intersection of pyroxene

HARDNESS:
6

SG:
3.7

LUSTER:
Vitreous

TRANSPARENCY:
Opaque

TESTS:
Restricted occurrence

LOOKALIKES:
Augite

Hedenbergite is a relatively uncommon calcium iron silicate occurring as a contact metamorphic mineral in skarns developed specifically between high-temperature igneous rocks and calcareous country rocks. It is usually associated with iron-rich silicates and other iron minerals in skarns. It also occurs in basic igneous rocks on the Moon.

FAMILY: PYROXENE

Hypersthene •
$(Mg,Fe)_2Si_2O_6$

Chemical group: Silicate

Hypersthene is a mixed iron-magnesium silicate that occurs in basic and intermediate igneous rocks such as norite and hypersthene-andesite. It also occurs widely in metamorphic rocks including high-grade regional charnockites and contact metamorphic hornfelses. Its subtle pink-green colors in thin section are distinctive. Basal prismatic sections show 90° cleavage intersection of pyroxene.

ID FACT FILE

CRYSTAL SYSTEM:
Orthorhombic

COLOR:
Brown, black, or greenish black

WHERE:
Igneous and metamorphic

ABUNDANCE:
Abundant

FORM:
Often massive, sometimes prismatic

CLEAVAGE:
Distinctive parallel along the length of crystals

HARDNESS:
5–6

SG:
3.4–3.5

LUSTER:
Submetallic

TRANSPARENCY:
Translucent to opaque

TESTS:
Diagnostic pyroxene cleavage. Uneven fracture, brittle

LOOKALIKES:
Bronzite distinguished by color and luster

FAMILY: PYROXENE

ID FACT FILE

CRYSTAL SYSTEM:
Monoclinic

COLOR:
Green, white

WHERE:
Metamorphic

ABUNDANCE:
Common

FORM:
Massive, fibrous

CLEAVAGE:
Imperfect

HARDNESS:
6.5–7

SG:
3.3–3.36

LUSTER:
Vitreous

TRANSPARENCY:
Translucent to
opaque

TESTS:
Uneven, brittle
fracture; very
tough. White
streak

LOOKALIKES:
Amphibole,
aegirine

Jadeite • NaAlSi$_2$O$_6$

Chemical group: Silicate

Jadeite is a variety of pyroxene and may have a composition partway toward aegirine. Its toughness and range of green colors are well known from its use as an ornamental and gemstone. It occurs in metamorphic schist, as in China, Japan, and in California. Jade is a common term used for semiprecious jadeite and another mineral with similar properties called nephrite (variety of actinolite). Photograph shows natural jadeite and a polished gem.

FAMILY: PYROXENOID

Pectolite •
$Ca_2NaH(SiO_3)_3$

Chemical group: Silicate

Pectolite is a fairly common white mineral occurring during hydrothermal alteration of igneous and volcanic rocks, such as in amygdales (gas-filled cavities or vesicles). It is usually associated with other zeolite minerals. It can also occur in igneous pegmatite. Radiating groups of elongated crystals are typical but easily mistaken for zeolites, especially where small crystal size requires use of a hand lens.

ID FACT FILE

CRYSTAL SYSTEM:
Monoclinic

COLOR:
White

WHERE:
Metamorphic, hydrothermal, igneous

ABUNDANCE:
Common

FORM:
Radiating, fibrous, or massive

CLEAVAGE:
Not prominent

HARDNESS:
5

SG:
2.7–2.9

LUSTER:
Silky when fibrous

TRANSPARENCY:
Opaque

TESTS:
White streak

LOOKALIKES:
Zeolite family

FAMILY: PYROXENOID

ID FACT FILE

CRYSTAL SYSTEM:
Triclinic

COLOR:
Pink, red;
oxidizes black

WHERE:
Metamorphic,
igneous

ABUNDANCE:
Restricted

FORM:
Massive, fibrous;
tabular crystals

CLEAVAGE:
Perfect

HARDNESS:
5.5–6.5

SG:
3.4–3.73

LUSTER:
Vitreous, pearly

TRANSPARENCY:
Translucent to
opaque

TESTS:
Uneven, brittle
fracture; tough
when massive.
White streak

LOOKALIKES:
Rose quartz,
rhodochrosite

Rhodonite • $Mn_2Si_2O_6$

Chemical group: Silicate

Crystals of rhodonite are rare. Its bright pink
to reddish color may be obscured by black
colors developed by oxidation. Impurities
commonly include some calcium and iron. It
occurs in hydrothermal vein systems
associated with lead-silver veins and other
manganese minerals, like rhodochrosite; also
in some metamorphic rocks like schist. It
occurs in France, India, the USA, and in the
Urals, in Russia. Less hard than quartz.

FAMILY: PYROXENE

ID FACT FILE

CRYSTAL SYSTEM:
Monoclinic

COLOR:
Gray, white, pale green, pink

WHERE:
Igneous

ABUNDANCE:
Restricted

FORM:
Prismatic, tabular crystals; also massive

CLEAVAGE:
Perfect

HARDNESS:
6–7

SG:
3.16–3.2

LUSTER:
Vitreous, pearly

TRANSPARENCY:
Transparent to translucent

TESTS:
Uneven fracture. White streak

LOOKALIKES:
Orthoclase

Spodumene • LiAlSi$_2$O$_6$

Chemical group: Silicate

Spodumene occurs in granite pegmatite, often accompanied by other lithium minerals like lepidolite and tourmaline. It may form large crystals with shiny cleavage surfaces. Transparent colored varieties used for gemstones are yellowish-green *hiddenite* and pink to violet *kunzite*. Photograph shows natural tabular crystal and cut gem.

FAMILY: PYROXENOID

Wollastonite • CaSiO₃

Chemical group: Silicate

ID FACT FILE

CRYSTAL SYSTEM:
Triclinic

COLOR:
White, gray, or brownish

WHERE:
Metamorphic and igneous

ABUNDANCE:
Common

FORM:
Tabular crystals, sometimes massive or fibrous

CLEAVAGE:
Obvious good cleavage

HARDNESS:
4.5–5

SG:
2.8–2.9

LUSTER:
Vitreous

TRANSPARENCY:
Translucent

TESTS:
Breaks rather easily along the cleavage

LOOKALIKES:
None

Wollastonite is a simple calcium silicate of the pyroxenoid family. It is always white or pale in color, often massive but can occur as tabular crystals. It occurs commonly in contact metamorphosed impure limestones and marbles. It also occurs in alkaline silicate volcanic rocks associated with carbonatites.

FAMILY: SERPENTINE

ID FACT FILE

CRYSTAL SYSTEM:
Monoclinic

COLOR:
Green, yellowish
green

WHERE:
Metamorphic

ABUNDANCE:
Rock-forming

FORM:
Crystals
unknown;
massive, scaly,
platy

CLEAVAGE:
Perfect

HARDNESS:
2.5–4

SG:
2.0–2.6

LUSTER:
Greasy, dull

TRANSPARENCY:
Translucent to
opaque

TESTS:
Conchoidal, flaky
fracture. White
streak. Massive
serpentine. Can
be cut with a
knife

LOOKALIKES:
Other serpentine
minerals

Antigorite •
$(Mg,Fe)_3Si_2O_5(OH)_4$

Chemical group: Hydrous magnesium silicate

The minerals *autigorite*, *lizardite*, and
chrysotile are structural variations (polymorphs)
of serpentine. Varieties rich in iron are darker
colored, often greenish. A massive variety with
dark reddish-brown to green colors is called
lizardite. It occurs in magnesium-rich
metamorphic rocks called serpentinite, usually
derived from ultrabasic igneous rocks rich in
olivine and pyroxene. Found in Cornwall in
England, Harz, in Germany, Cyprus, Eastern
Canada, South Africa, and Zimbabwe.

FAMILY: SERPENTINE

Chrysotile •
$Mg_3Si_2O_5(OH)_4$

Chemical group: Hydrous magnesium silicate

ID FACT FILE

CRYSTAL SYSTEM:
Monoclinic

COLOR:
Green, gray,
white

WHERE:
Metamorphic

ABUNDANCE:
Rock-forming

FORM:
Crystals
unknown; fibrous
aggregates,
asbestos

CLEAVAGE:
Perfect,
separable fibres

HARDNESS:
2.5–4

SG:
2.0–2.6

LUSTER:
Greasy, dull

TRANSPARENCY:
Translucent to
opaque

TESTS:
Splintery
fracture. White
streak

LOOKALIKES:
Distinctive
fibrous mineral

Chrysotile is the fibrous form of serpentine, with fine or coarse fibers occurring in veins and lenses in massive varieties of metamorphic serpentine (serpentinite rock). Aggregates with parallel fibers are called *asbestos*. The mineral also occurs in veins in some impure marbles. Impurities can include small amounts of iron and manganese. Found in Cornwall in England, Harz, in Germany, Cyprus, Eastern Canada, South Africa, and Zimbabwe. Photograph shows asbestos chrysotile.

ID FACT FILE

CRYSTAL SYSTEM:
Trigonal

COLOR:
White, bluish, colored

WHERE:
Sedimentary, igneous

ABUNDANCE:
Abundant

FORM:
Microcrystalline varieties of quartz; fibrous, massive

CLEAVAGE:
None

HARDNESS:
6.5–7

SG:
2.58–2.65

LUSTER:
Waxy, dull

TRANSPARENCY:
Translucent

TESTS:
Conchoidal fracture. White streak. Crystals not visible to naked eye. Porous and permeable by dyes

LOOKALIKES:
Zeolites

Quartz-chalcedony • SiO_2

Chemical group: Silica

The many forms of chalcedony are all varieties of microcrystalline quartz, often partly hydrated. Crystals are not visible. They occur as nodules in sedimentary rocks, and as infilling of cavities in igneous rocks and mineralized vein systems. *Carnelian* is translucent yellowish red; *jasper* is brown-red or rarely green; *bloodstone* is bright green speckled with red; *agate* is composed of different colored bands; *flint* is black to gray, and *chert* is similar but lacking conchoidal fracture.

FAMILY: QUARTZ

ID FACT FILE

CRYSTAL SYSTEM:
Trigonal

COLOR:
White, various colors; opalescent

WHERE:
Sedimentary, igneous

ABUNDANCE:
Uncommon

FORM:
Microcrystalline varieties of quartz; fibrous, massive

CLEAVAGE:
None

HARDNESS:
5.5–6

SG:
1.98–2.5

LUSTER:
Vitreous, greasy

TRANSPARENCY:
Transparent to opaque

TESTS:
Conchoidal fracture. White streak. Crystals not visible to naked eye

LOOKALIKES:
Quartz-chalcedony

Opal • $SiO_2.nH_2O$

Chemical group: Hydrous silica

Opal lacks almost any crystalline structure (amorphous). It contains up to 30 percent water, and is lighter and softer than quartz. It occurs filling fractures in igneous rocks and as crusts and nodules in sedimentary rocks. There are many variety names and colors and most show an internal play of colors with rainbow tints called opalescence (as illustrated); common opal, *hyalite*, is glassy and almost colorless; *precious opal*, like *fire-opal*, shows spectacular opalescence. Gem-quality opal is obtained from Mexico and especially from Australia.

FAMILY: QUARTZ

ID FACT FILE

CRYSTAL SYSTEM:
Trigonal

COLOR:
Colorless, white

WHERE:
Igneous, metamorphic, sedimentary

ABUNDANCE:
Rock-forming

FORM:
Pointed, six-sided prismatic crystals; also massive

CLEAVAGE:
None

HARDNESS:
7

SG:
2.65

LUSTER:
Vitreous, greasy

TRANSPARENCY:
Transparent to opaque

TESTS:
Conchoidal fracture. White streak

LOOKALIKES:
Feldspars

Quartz • SiO$_2$

Chemical group: Silica

Quartz is the second most abundant rock-forming mineral after feldspar. It occurs widely in silica-rich igneous rocks like granite. There are several different polymorphs of quartz; in high-temperature igneous rocks it forms *tridymite* (*see* opposite) and *cristobalite*; in very high-pressure impact metamorphic rocks it forms *coesite* and *stishovite*. It is resistant to weathering and accumulates in sands as well as in sedimentary rocks like sandstone. It is widely distributed in metamorphic rocks like gneiss, migmatite, and quartzite. Quartz also occurs as a prominent matrix mineral in hydrothermal vein systems. There are many named varieties of quartz, due to its different colors and forms; *rock crystal* is colorless, *amethyst* is purple, and *citrine* is yellow (*see* opposite).

FAMILY: QUARTZ

Top: Tridymite
Middle left: Citrine, cut gem
Middle right: Amethyst
Bottom: Twins

FAMILY: ZEOLITE

Analcime •
$NaAlSi_2O_6.H_2O$

Chemical group: Hydrous silicate

ID FACT FILE

CRYSTAL SYSTEM:
Monoclinic or cubic

COLOR:
Milky white, tints of pale green, yellow, or pink

WHERE:
Igneous

ABUNDANCE:
Abundant

FORM:
Equant crystals; granular aggregates

CLEAVAGE:
None

HARDNESS:
5–5.5

SG:
2.24–2.31

LUSTER:
Vitreous

TRANSPARENCY:
Transparent to opaque

TESTS:
Conchoidal, uneven fracture. White streak

LOOKALIKES:
Nepheline

Analcime occurs as a primary mineral in some alkaline igneous rocks like dolerite, alkali basalt, and phonolite. It also occurs in typical zeolitic form as a secondary hydrous alteration of feldspars and feldspathoids, filling cavities, cracks, and spaces in volcanic lavas and other igneous rocks. Found in Scotland, Ireland, Germany, France, and Mt. St. Hilaire, Quebec.

FAMILY: APOPHYLLITE

Apophyllite* •
$KCa_4Si_8O_{20}F.8H_2O$

Chemical group: Hydrous silicate

Apophyllite is a fairly common mineral
growing as clusters of crystals protruding into
voids in lava flows. It also occurs in some
hydrothermal mineral veins. It often occurs
together with other zeolite minerals in
hydrothermally altered basalts as in Scotland,
Germany, and Poona, Mumbai, in India.

*Apophyllite often contains chlorine in place
of some fluorine; depending on which is
dominant it is more accurately called
fluorapophyllite or chlorapophyllite.

FAMILY: ZEOLITE

Harmotome • $(Ba,K)\sim_2$ $(Si,Al)_8O_{16}.6H_2O$

Chemical group: Hydrous silicate

ID FACT FILE

CRYSTAL SYSTEM:
Monoclinic

COLOR:
White, gray

WHERE:
Igneous

ABUNDANCE:
Common

FORM:
Prismatic
crystals, cross-
like twinning

CLEAVAGE:
Imperfect

HARDNESS:
4.5

SG:
2.44–2.50

LUSTER:
Vitreous

TRANSPARENCY:
Translucent,
cloudy

TESTS:
Uneven, brittle
fracture. White
streak

LOOKALIKES:
Analcime,
zeolites

Harmotome is a potassium-rich zeolite, usually
with some barium. It occurs in hydrothermal
mineral veins associated with other barium- or
strontium-rich minerals, as at Strontian in
Scotland. As with other zeolites it also occurs
as secondary infillings in voids, cracks, and
veins in altered volcanic rocks. Found in Idar-
Oberstein and Harz in Germany, Kongsberg,
in Norway, and in France and Italy.

FAMILY: ZEOLITE

Heulandite • $(Ca,Na)_{2-3}$ $Al_3(Al,Si)_2Si_{13}O_{36}.12H_2O$

Chemical group: Hydrous silicate

ID FACT FILE

CRYSTAL SYSTEM:
Monoclinic

COLOR:
White, red, brown

WHERE:
Igneous, metamorphic

ABUNDANCE:
Common

FORM:
Tabular crystals, lamellar aggregates, radiating; globular

CLEAVAGE:
Perfect

HARDNESS:
3.5–4

SG:
2.2

LUSTER:
Vitreous

TRANSPARENCY:
Transparent to translucent

TESTS:
Uneven, brittle fracture. White streak

LOOKALIKES:
Zeolites

Heulandite is a calcium-sodium-rich zeolite, sometimes with minor barium or strontium. As with other zeolites it occurs as secondary infillings in voids, cracks, and veins in altered volcanic rocks. It also occurs in veins in metamorphic rocks, and in hydrothermal mineral veins. Found in Scotland, Ireland, Idar-Oberstein and Harz, in Germany, Kongsberg, in Norway, Iceland, France, and in the state of Idaho. The photograph shows enlargement of small crystals lining a volcanic cavity.

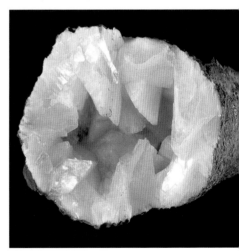

FAMILY: ZEOLITE

Mesolite • Na_2Ca_2 $Al_6Si_9O_{30}.8H_2O$

Chemical group: Hydrous silicate

ID FACT FILE

CRYSTAL SYSTEM:
Monoclinic

COLOR:
Colorless, white

WHERE:
Igneous,
metamorphic

ABUNDANCE:
Abundant

FORM:
Long prismatic
crystals, fibrous,
radiating
aggregates

CLEAVAGE:
Perfect

HARDNESS:
5

SG:
2–2.4

LUSTER:
Vitreous, silky

TRANSPARENCY:
Transparent to
translucent

TESTS:
Conchoidal,
brittle fracture.
White streak

LOOKALIKES:
Zeolites

Mesolite is a zeolite with approximately equal sodium and calcium. It typically forms long slender crystals. As with other zeolites it can also occur as secondary infillings in voids, gas cavities, cracks, and veins in altered volcanic rocks. Found in Antrim, in Ireland, Faeroes, Iceland, Skye and Mull, in Scotland, Auvergne, in France, and Cheyenne, Wyoming.

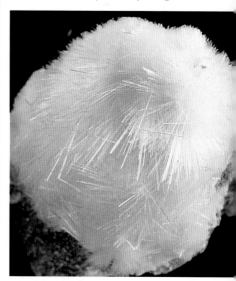

FAMILY: ZEOLITE

Natrolite •
$Na_2Al_2Si_3O_{10} \cdot 2H_2O$

Chemical group:Hydrous silicate

ID FACT FILE

CRYSTAL SYSTEM:
Orthorhombic

COLOR:
White

WHERE:
Igneous,
metamorphic

ABUNDANCE:
Abundant

FORM:
Needlelike
crystals, fibrous,
radiating
aggregates

CLEAVAGE:
Perfect

HARDNESS:
5–5.5

SG:
2.2–2.25

LUSTER:
Vitreous, pearly

TRANSPARENCY:
Transparent to
translucent

TESTS:
Conchoidal,
brittle fracture.
White streak

LOOKALIKES:
Zeolites

Natrolite is a sodium-rich zeolite that forms
needle-shaped crystals. As with other zeolites it
occurs widely as secondary infillings in voids,
cracks, and veins in altered volcanic rocks. Also
occurs in hydrothermal mineral veins. Found
in Antrim, in Ireland, Scotland, Idar-Oberstein
and Harz, in Germany, Iceland, Auvergne, in
France, and in San Benito, California.

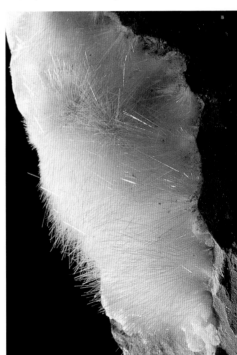

FAMILY: PREHNITE

Prehnite • $Ca_2Al_2Si_3O_{10} \cdot (OH)_2$

Chemical group:Hydrous calcium aluminum silicate

ID FACT FILE

CRYSTAL SYSTEM:
Orthorhombic

COLOR:
Pale green, white

WHERE:
Metamorphic

ABUNDANCE:
Common

FORM:
Soft white clay; rarely small hexagonal crystals

CLEAVAGE:
Imperfect

HARDNESS:
6–6.5

SG:
2.8–3.0

LUSTER:
Vitreous, pearly

TRANSPARENCY:
Transparent to translucent

TESTS:
Uneven fracture. White streak

LOOKALIKES:
Feldspar

Prehnite forms globular masses with radiating crystal structures in cavities, and also as rare tabular slightly curved crystals. It often has a distinctive pale green color. It occurs in cavities in igneous lavas often with zeolite minerals. It can be abundant in some metamorphic schists and calc silicate rocks. Found in Idar-Oberstein and Harzburg, in Germany, Dauphiné, in France, Kilpatrick and Campsie Hills, in Scotland, and Bou Arta, in Morocco.

FAMILY: ZEOLITE

Stilbite • $NaCa_2Al_5Si_{13}O_{36} \cdot 14H_2O$

Chemical group: Hydrous silicate

ID FACT FILE

CRYSTAL SYSTEM:
Monoclinic

COLOR:
White, yellowish, reddish

WHERE:
Igneous, metamorphic

ABUNDANCE:
Abundant

FORM:
Thin tabular crystals, radiating sheaf-like aggregates

CLEAVAGE:
Perfect

HARDNESS:
3.5–4

SG:
2.1–2.2

LUSTER:
Vitreous, pearly

TRANSPARENCY:
Transparent to translucent

TESTS:
Uneven, brittle fracture. White streak

LOOKALIKES:
Zeolites

Stilbite is a sodium- and calcium-rich zeolite that can form characteristic sheaflike bunches of crystals. As with other zeolites it occurs widely as secondary infillings in voids, cracks, and veins in altered volcanic rocks; rather common infilling gas escape cavities in Tertiary basaltic lavas of Antrim, in Ireland. Also occurs in hydrothermal mineral veins. Found in Skye and Mull, in Scotland, Harz, in Germany, Faeroes, Iceland, Auvergne, in France, Nova Scotia, in Canada, and Crestmore, California.

ID FACT FILE

CRYSTAL SYSTEM:
Orthorhombic

COLOR:
Colorless, gray, reddish

WHERE:
Metamorphic

ABUNDANCE:
Rock-forming

FORM:
Squarish prismatic crystals; also granular, massive

CLEAVAGE:
Poor

HARDNESS:
7.5

SG:
3.1–3.3

LUSTER:
Vitreous, dull

TRANSPARENCY:
Transparent to opaque

TESTS:
Uneven, brittle fracture. White streak

LOOKALIKES:
Orthoclase

Andalusite • Al_2SiO_5

Chemical group: Alumino-silicate

Andalusite occurs in metamorphic rocks including regional gneiss and schist; it also occurs in contact metamorphic rocks adjacent to high-temperature igneous intrusions. Many cross-sections have a characteristic square shape. The variety *chiastolite* reveals a distinctive internal black crosslike structure set in whitish or gray crystals with squarish outlines. It is widespread and found in Cumberland, in England and Andalucia, in Spain. Impurities can include sodium, potassium, and manganese.

FAMILY: BERYL

ID FACT FILE

CRYSTAL SYSTEM:
Hexagonal

COLOR:
Green, blue,
yellow, white

WHERE:
Igneous,
metamorphic,
sedimentary

ABUNDANCE:
Common

FORM:
Tabular crystals,
often twinned;
also massive,
granular

CLEAVAGE:
Imperfect

HARDNESS:
7.5–8

SG:
2.6–2.9

LUSTER:
Vitreous

TRANSPARENCY:
Transparent to
opaque

TESTS:
Conchoidal,
uneven fracture.
White streak

LOOKALIKES:
Tourmaline

Beryl • $Be_3Al_2Si_6O_{18}$

Chemical group: Silicate

Beryl in its unattractive cloudy form is the chief
source of the element beryllium. It occurs as
six-sided prismatic crystals in minor quantities in
acid igneous rocks like granite and forms larger
prismatic crystals in pegmatite. Precious beryl is
beautiful and includes several varieties used for
gems. *Emerald* is the famous green variety from
pegmatites in Austria, Colombia, Zimbabwe, and
South Africa. *Aquamarine* is the pale blue
variety from pegmatite and granite as in Mourne
Mountains, in Ireland, Brazil, and Madagascar.
Chrysoberyl is a completely different tabular
mineral (Al_2BeO_4) from pegmatites and schists
known for the red-green gem variety *alexandrite*.

FAMILY: CHLORITE

Chlorite* • $(Fe, Mg, Mn, Al)_6(Si, Al)_4O_{10} \cdot (OH, O)_8$

Chemical group: Hydrous silicate

ID FACT FILE

CRYSTAL SYSTEM:
Monoclinic

COLOR:
Green, greenish black

WHERE:
Igneous, metamorphic

ABUNDANCE:
Rock-forming

FORM:
Tabular crystals, granular; scaly aggregates

CLEAVAGE:
Perfect

HARDNESS:
2–3

SG:
2.6–3.4

LUSTER:
Pearly

TRANSPARENCY:
Translucent to opaque

TESTS:
Flaky fracture. Scratched by fingernail. Gray-green streak

LOOKALIKES:
Actinolite, amphibole

*Chlorite is the name for a group of common, even rock-forming minerals, generally of greenish color. The important chlorite minerals are the magnesium-iron-rich *chamosite* and *clinochlore*, followed by an oxidized chlorite called *delessite* and a manganese-rich variety *pennantite*. It occurs widely as a secondary mineral in igneous rocks. It is a rock-forming mineral in metamorphic rocks like chlorite-schist.

Chrysocolla • $CuSiO_3.nH_2O$

Chemical group: Hydrous copper silicate

ID FACT FILE

CRYSTAL SYSTEM:
Amorphous

COLOR:
Bluish green, whitish green, turquoise

WHERE:
Igneous

ABUNDANCE:
Restricted

FORM:
Globular, massive, gel-like

CLEAVAGE:
None

HARDNESS:
2–4

SG:
2–2.2

LUSTER:
Vitreous, greasy

TRANSPARENCY:
Translucent to opaque

TESTS:
Conchoidal, brittle fracture. White or greenish streak

LOOKALIKES:
Azurite, malachite

Chrysocolla is a distinctive pale to vivid green copper mineral. It contains a variable amount of water, and additional impurities like aluminum. Crystalline forms are unknown, and its apparent lack of internal structure is called amorphous. It commonly occurs in association with other copper minerals in the weathering zone of copper deposits, as in Cornwall and the Lake District, in England, Nizhne-Tagilsk, in the Urals, in Russia, and in Copiapo, in Chile.

ID FACT FILE

CRYSTAL SYSTEM:
Orthorhombic

COLOR:
Blue, violet, gray

WHERE:
Metamorphic,
igneous

ABUNDANCE:
Rock-forming

FORM:
Crystals rare;
massive
aggregates

CLEAVAGE:
Imperfect

HARDNESS:
7–7.5

SG:
2.5–2.7

LUSTER:
Vitreous, greasy

TRANSPARENCY:
Transparent to
translucent

TESTS:
Conchoidal,
uneven fracture.
Bluish-white
streak

LOOKALIKES:
Andalusite

Cordierite •
$(Mg,Fe)_2Al_4Si_5O_{18}$

Chemical group: Alumino-silicate

This alumino-silicate often has a characteristic
violet-blue color but rarely forms distinct
crystals. It occurs widely in regional
metamorphic rocks, like cordierite-gneiss, and
in contact metamorphic rocks like cordierite
hornfels; often associated with andalusite. It
can also be a minor constituent of some large
igneous bodies like norite which have been
contaminated by sedimentary rocks.

FAMILY: CHRYSOCOLLA

Dioptase • CuSiO$_2$.(OH)$_2$

Chemical group: Hydrous copper silicate

ID FACT FILE

CRYSTAL SYSTEM:
Trigonal

COLOR:
Vivid emerald-green

WHERE:
Igneous

ABUNDANCE:
Uncommon

FORM:
Stubby crystals; rhombic faces

CLEAVAGE:
Perfect

HARDNESS:
5

SG:
3.28–3.35

LUSTER:
Vitreous

TRANSPARENCY:
Transparent to translucent

TESTS:
Conchoidal, brittle fracture. Green streak

LOOKALIKES:
Unlikely to be mistaken

Dioptase occurs as distinctive emerald-green crystals encrusting surfaces and lining cavities in the weathering zone of copper deposits. It is often associated with copper carbonate minerals and calcite. It is rather uncommon but easily recognized by its color and well developed rhomb-shaped crystal faces. Found in Kazakhstan, in Russia, in the state of Arizona, in Chile, and in Zaire.

FAMILY: EPIDOTE

Epidote • Ca$_2$(Al, Fe)$_3$(SiO$_4$)$_3$OH

Chemical group: Silicate

ID FACT FILE

CRYSTAL SYSTEM:
Monoclinic

COLOR:
Green, yellowish green, black, red°

WHERE:
Metamorphic, igneous

ABUNDANCE:
Rock-forming

FORM:
Prismatic crystals, striated; also granular, massive

CLEAVAGE:
Perfect

HARDNESS:
6–7

SG:
3.3–3.5

LUSTER:
Vitreous

TRANSPARENCY:
Transparent to opaque

TESTS:
Conchoidal, uneven fracture. Gray streak

LOOKALIKES:
Olivine, augite

Epidote is an abundant and widespread metamorphic mineral occurring in calcium-rich rocks derived from impure limestones or igneous rocks. It also occurs in some igneous rocks like granite. *Clinozoisite* is a pale-colored mineral in the epidote group with little iron; it occurs as a secondary mineral in metamorphosed igneous rocks. *Piemontite°* is a distinctive red mineral in the epidote group with high manganese and occurs in schists.

FAMILY: HEMIMORPHITE

Hemimorphite •
$Zn_4Si_2O_7.(OH)_2.H_2O$

Chemical group: Hydrous zinc silicate

ID FACT FILE

CRYSTAL SYSTEM:
Orthorhombic

COLOR:
White, brownish,
pale green, or
blue

WHERE:
Igneous

ABUNDANCE:
Restricted

FORM:
Small tabular
crystals; also
massive,
globular

CLEAVAGE:
Perfect

HARDNESS:
5

SG:
3.3–3.5

LUSTER:
Vitreous

TRANSPARENCY:
Transparent to
translucent

TESTS:
Conchoidal,
brittle fracture.
White streak

LOOKALIKES:
Malachite,
chrysocolla

Hemimorphite is a common zinc mineral often with tabular crystals. It occurs in the weathering or oxidation zone of lead-zinc deposits where it can be accompanied by similar-colored zinc carbonate (*smithsonite*). It is an important source of zinc. Found in Cumberland and Derbyshire, in England, in Austria, Russia, and Arizona. Uncommon pale green massive forms may be mistaken for green copper minerals, but the presence of any crystals is distinctive.

FAMILY: KAOLINITE

ID FACT FILE

CRYSTAL SYSTEM:
Triclinic

COLOR:
White

WHERE:
Igneous

ABUNDANCE:
Abundant

FORM:
Soft white clay;
rarely small
hexagonal
crystals

CLEAVAGE:
Perfect

HARDNESS:
2–2.5

SG:
2.6

LUSTER:
Dull

TRANSPARENCY:
Translucent to
opaque

TESTS:
Feels greasy.
Crumbles to
powder

LOOKALIKES:
Other clay
minerals

Kaolinite •
$Al_2Si_2O_5.(OH)_4$

Chemical group: Hydrous aluminum silicate

Kaolinite is a white common clay mineral typically formed by alteration of feldspar in granite. It is soft and easily scratched with a fingernail. It may be associated with other minerals like tourmaline and cassiterite in hydrothermally altered granite and greisen. It is locally abundant and even rock-forming; it is extracted for commercial use, as in Cornwall, in England and in France. The photograph shows kaolinite in the shape of orthoclase crystals; such replacements are called pseudomorphs.

FAMILY: KYANITE

ID FACT FILE

CRYSTAL SYSTEM:
Triclinic

COLOR:
Light blue, rarely other colors

WHERE:
Metamorphic

ABUNDANCE:
Rock-forming

FORM:
Long bladed crystals

CLEAVAGE:
Perfect

HARDNESS:
4–7 (variable)

SG:
3.6–3.7

LUSTER:
Vitreous, pearly

TRANSPARENCY:
Transparent to translucent

TESTS:
Fibrous, brittle fracture. White streak

LOOKALIKES:
Unlikely to be mistaken

Kyanite • Al_2SiO_5

Chemical group: Alumino-silicate

The blue color and variation in hardness (hardest across the base of crystals) are distinctive. Kyanite occurs as rulerlike crystals widely distributed in high-grade metamorphic rocks like gneiss, micaschist, and eclogite, as in Scotland and in Switzerland. Kyanite has the same composition as both sillimanite and andalusite. It can contain impurities of sodium, potassium, and chromium.

ID FACT FILE

CRYSTAL SYSTEM:
Tetragonal

COLOR:
Colorless, white, gray, brown

WHERE:
Igneous

ABUNDANCE:
Rock-forming

FORM:
Short prismatic or tabular crystals

CLEAVAGE:
Imperfect

HARDNESS:
5–5.5

SG:
2.9–3.1

LUSTER:
Vitreous to pearly

TRANSPARENCY:
Transparent to translucent

TESTS:
Uneven, brittle fracture. White or gray streak

LOOKALIKES:
Feldspar, wollastonite

FAMILY: MELILITE

Melilite* • $Ca_2MgSi_2O_7$ to $CaAl_2SiO_7$

Chemical group: Silicate

*Melilite is the name for a mineral group with any composition between the pure magnesium *akermanite* and pure aluminum *gehlenite*; it can be either a mafic or a leucocratic mineral. It is an important constituent of alkaline basic igneous rocks like melilite-basalt and nephelinite. Igneous rocks comprised of mostly melilite are called *melilitite* (volcanic) or *melilitolite* (plutonic); they often occur in association with carbonatite. Melilite is a common mineral in chondrite meteorites.

FAMILY: PYROPHYLLITE

Pyrophyllite •
$Al_2Si_4O_{10} \cdot (OH)_2$

Chemical group: Hydrous aluminum silicate

ID FACT FILE

CRYSTAL SYSTEM:
Monoclinic or triclinic

COLOR:
White, gray, greenish

WHERE:
Metamorphic, igneous

ABUNDANCE:
Common

FORM:
Radiating aggregates, massive; tabular crystals

CLEAVAGE:
Perfect

HARDNESS:
1–1.5

SG:
2.66–2.90

LUSTER:
Vitreous, pearly

TRANSPARENCY:
Transparent to translucent

TESTS:
Uneven fracture, flexible. White streak. Feels greasy

LOOKALIKES:
Talc

Pyrophyllite is similar in many ways to talc, but can form more distinctive crystalline aggregates, with elongated tabular shapes. It is very soft and easily scratched with a fingernail. It occurs mainly as lenses and beds in metamorphic schists, and also in some hydrothermal mineral veins. Locally rock-forming deposits are mined for industrial use. Found in Eifel, in Germany, in Belgium, in Luxembourg, in Finland, North Carolina, Georgia, and California and in South Africa.

FAMILY: SCAPOLITE

ID FACT FILE

CRYSTAL SYSTEM:
Tetragonal

COLOR:
Colorless, white,
gray, brown

WHERE:
Metamorphic

ABUNDANCE:
Abundant

FORM:
Prismatic
crystals; also
massive,
granular

CLEAVAGE:
Perfect

HARDNESS:
5–6.5

SG:
2.54–2.77

LUSTER:
Vitreous, greasy

TRANSPARENCY:
Transparent to
opaque

TESTS:
Conchoidal,
brittle fracture.
White streak

LOOKALIKES:
Feldspar

Scapolite* •
$3NaAlSi_3O_8.NaCl$ to
$3CaAl_2Si_2O_6.CaCO_3$

Chemical group: Silicate

*Scapolite is the name for a mineral group
with any composition between the pure
sodium *marialite* and pure calcium *meionite*;
common scapolite has a mixed composition
somewhere between these two ideal types. It
is a pale-colored mineral. It occurs as an
alteration product of plagioclase feldspar in
igneous rocks, but more commonly in
metamorphic rocks like marble, gneiss,
amphibolite, and granulite.

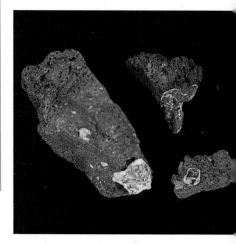

FAMILY: SILLIMANITE

ID FACT FILE

CRYSTAL SYSTEM:
Orthorhombic

COLOR:
Gray, brownish, greenish

WHERE:
Metamorphic

ABUNDANCE:
Rock-forming

FORM:
Needle-shaped crystals, radiating, fibrous aggregates

CLEAVAGE:
Perfect

HARDNESS:
3.2–3.3

SG:
6.5–7

LUSTER:
Vitreous, greasy

TRANSPARENCY:
Transparent to translucent

TESTS:
Uneven fracture. White streak

LOOKALIKES:
Rutile

Sillimanite • Al_2SiO_5

Chemical group: Alumino-silicate

Sillimanite is a common alumino-silicate mineral with a very elongated crystal form. It usually occurs as felted aggregates in metamorphic rocks, including contact metamorphosed hornfels. Also occurs widely in regional high-grade metamorphic rocks like gneiss, micaschist, granulite, and eclogite as in Finland, Germany, Norway, Scotland, and Switzerland. Though it is often abundant, its small granular size can make it difficult to recognize, even with the use of a hand lens.

FAMILY: STAUROLITE

Staurolite • $(Fe,Mg,Zn)_2$ $Al_9(Si,Al)_4O_{22}(OH)_2$

Chemical group: Alumino-silicate

ID FACT FILE

CRYSTAL SYSTEM:
Orthorhombic

COLOR:
Brown, black

WHERE:
Metamorphic

ABUNDANCE:
Common

FORM:
Stout prismatic crystals, often twinned like a cross or a tilted cross

CLEAVAGE:
Imperfect

HARDNESS:
7–7.5

SG:
3.65–3.77

LUSTER:
Vitreous

TRANSPARENCY:
Translucent to opaque

TESTS:
Conchoidal fracture. White streak

LOOKALIKES:
Cross unlikely to be mistaken

Staurolite is a metamorphic mineral often associated with kyanite and garnet in aluminum-rich rocks like gneiss and mica-schist. Crystals usually have a dull, rough, slightly pitted surface. Occasionally also occurs as resistant heavy mineral in sedimentary sands. May contain some sodium. The cruciform shape combined with high hardness and dark color are distinctive features.

FAMILY: TALC

ID FACT FILE

CRYSTAL SYSTEM:
Monoclinic

COLOR:
Colorless, white, greenish

WHERE:
Metamorphic

ABUNDANCE:
Rock-forming

FORM:
Massive, scaly, granular

CLEAVAGE:
Perfect

HARDNESS:
1

SG:
2.7–2.8

LUSTER:
Pearly, greasy

TRANSPARENCY:
Transparent to opaque

TESTS:
Flexible. Feels greasy or soapy. White streak

LOOKALIKES:
Serpentine

Talc • $Mg_3Si_4O_{10}(OH)_2$

Chemical group: Hydrous magnesium silicate

Talc has distinctive low hardness; it is the softest mineral in the Moh's scale of hardness (=1). It has a soapy feel. It occurs in hydrous altered magnesium-rich igneous rocks like serpentinite, and in contact metamorphic zones around granite bodies. It is locally common in some metamorphosed limestones, and is a rock-forming mineral in some schists, as in Germany, Austria, Scotland, and Italy. The photograph is an enlargement of the scaly form.

FAMILY: TITANITE

ID FACT FILE

CRYSTAL SYSTEM:
Monoclinic

COLOR:
Brown, yellow, green, black

WHERE:
Igneous

ABUNDANCE:
Common

FORM:
Prismatic crystals, wedge- or lozenge-shaped

CLEAVAGE:
Imperfect

HARDNESS:
5–5.5

SG:
3.4–3.6

LUSTER:
Greasy

TRANSPARENCY:
Transparent to opaque

TESTS:
Conchoidal, brittle fracture

LOOKALIKES:
Zircon

Titanite • $CaTiSiO_5$

Chemical group: Silicate

Titanite (old name sphene) occurs in small quantities in many coarse-grained igneous rocks like diorite, granite, and granodiorite. It is an important host for titanium (Ti), but impurities may also include small amounts of zirconium, lanthanum, and cerium. It is distinguished from zircon by its more angular shape and lower hardness.

Topaz •
$Ca_2Fe_5Si_8O_{22}(OH)_2$
Chemical group: Silicate

ID FACT FILE

CRYSTAL SYSTEM:
Orthorhombic

COLOR:
Straw-yellow, brown, colorless

WHERE:
Igneous

ABUNDANCE:
Common

FORM:
Prismatic crystals

CLEAVAGE:
Perfect

HARDNESS:
8

SG:
3.5–3.6

LUSTER:
Vitreous

TRANSPARENCY:
Transparent to translucent

TESTS:
White streak. Conchoidal, uneven fracture

LOOKALIKES:
Zircon

Topaz is a hard mineral that occurs in acid igneous rocks like granite. It also occurs in hydrothermal veins with tin minerals, as in Cornwall, in England. Good crystals can be found protruding into cavities in some granite, as in Mourne Mountains, in Ireland; also in greisen and especially pegmatite. Uncommon pink or blue forms are used as gemstones, usually from sedimentary placer deposits, as in the Urals in Russia and in Brazil; color may be modified by heating. The photograph shows a natural crystal and a cut gem.

FAMILY: VESUVIANITE

ID FACT FILE

CRYSTAL SYSTEM:
Tetragonal

COLOR:
Brown, green, yellow

WHERE:
Igneous, metamorphic, sedimentary

ABUNDANCE:
Rock-forming

FORM:
Equant stubby crystals, often twinned; also massive.

CLEAVAGE:
Poor

HARDNESS:
6.5

SG:
3.3–3.45

LUSTER:
Vitreous, greasy

TRANSPARENCY:
Transparent to opaque

TESTS:
Uneven, splintery fracture. White streak

LOOKALIKES:
Zircon, melilite

Vesuvianite • $Ca_{10}(Mg, Fe)_2Al_4Si_9O_{34}(OH)_4$

Chemical group: Silicate

Vesuvianite is a complex silicate which occurs widely in metamorphic rocks such as marble, calcium-silicate hornfels, and serpentinite; as in Tyrol, in Austria, Zermatt, in Switzerland, and in the Dolomites, in Italy. Well-formed crystals often occur in heat-metamorphosed limestone, as in blocks from Mt. Vesuvius, in Italy. It is distinguished from zircon by its lower hardness (scratched by quartz), and from melilite by its stubby shape.

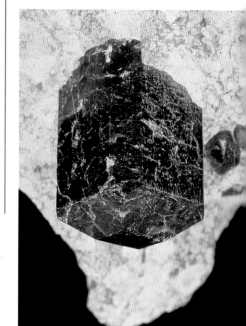

FAMILY: ZIRCON

ID FACT FILE

CRYSTAL SYSTEM:
Tetragonal

COLOR:
Brown, red,
yellow

WHERE:
Igneous,
metamorphic,
sedimentary

ABUNDANCE:
Abundant

FORM:
Stubby prisms,
rounded grains

CLEAVAGE:
Poor

HARDNESS:
7–7.5

SG:
4.7

LUSTER:
Greasy

TRANSPARENCY:
Transparent to
opaque

TESTS:
White streak.
Conchoidal brittle
fracture

LOOKALIKES:
Topaz

Zircon • ZrSiO$_4$

Chemical group: Silicate

Zircon is the most important source of the
element zirconium; it can also contain hafnium.
It occurs in small amounts in a wide variety of
igneous rocks, from volcanic kimberlite and
andesite to coarse-grained granite, nepheline
syenite, and pegmatite. It also occurs in
metamorphic rocks like gneiss. It is resistant to
weathering and occurs widely in sedimentary
rocks as a "heavy mineral"; sometimes
concentrated in beach sands and mined, as in
Australia and Brazil. The photograph shows a
group of collected crystals, much enlarged.

FAMILY: EPIDOTE

ID FACT FILE

CRYSTAL SYSTEM:
Orthorhombic

COLOR:
White, gray,
green, blue,
pink°

WHERE:
Metamorphic

ABUNDANCE:
Abundant

FORM:
Prismatic,
striated crystals;
massive
aggregates

CLEAVAGE:
Perfect

HARDNESS:
6–6.5

SG:
3.2–3.37

LUSTER:
Vitreous

TRANSPARENCY:
Transparent to
opaque

TESTS:
Conchoidal,
splintery fracture.
White streak

LOOKALIKES:
Pyroxene,
wollastonite

Zoisite •
$Ca_2Al_3(SiO_4)_3OH$

Chemical group: Silicate

Zoisite is an alumino-silicate that occurs
commonly in metamorphic rocks derived from
igneous rocks with calcium-rich feldspar, like
amphibolite. Impurities can include
manganese, which gives a rose-pink color in
the variety *thulite*. *Tanzanite* is a distinctive
blue color and is used as a gemstone; it is only
known from gneisses in northern Tanzania.

Axinite • (Ca,Mn,Fe) Al₂BSi₄O₁₅(OH)

$$(Ca,Mn,Fe)Al_2BSi_4O_{15}(OH)$$

Chemical group: Boro-silicate

ID FACT FILE

Crystal system:
Triclinic

Color:
Brown, gray,
violet, green

Where:
Metamorphic,
igneous

Abundance:
Common

Form:
Tabular or
wedge-shaped
crystals

Cleavage:
Perfect

Hardness:
6.5–7

SG:
3.3–3.4

Luster:
3.3–3.4

Transparency:
Transparent to
translucent

Tests:
Choncoidal,
brittle fracture.
White streak

Lookalikes:
Titanite

Axinite is a silicate with essential boron (B), a boro-silicate. It usually forms thin and very sharp edged, axelike crystals. It occurs in contact metamorphic rocks around granites and in cavities within granite, as in Cornwall, in England. It may be associated with other boro-silicate minerals like tourmaline. It also occurs in calc silicate hornfels as in Harz, in Germany and Dauphiné, in France.

FAMILY: GADOLINITE

ID FACT FILE

CRYSTAL SYSTEM:
Monoclinic

COLOR:
Colorless, pale
yellow, or green

WHERE:
Igneous,
metamorphic

ABUNDANCE:
Restricted

FORM:
Stubby prismatic
or tabular
crystals; massive

CLEAVAGE:
None

HARDNESS:
5–5.5

SG:
2.9–3.0

LUSTER:
Vitreous, greasy

TRANSPARENCY:
Transparent to
translucent

TESTS:
Conchoidal
fracture. White
streak

LOOKALIKES:
Wollastonite

Datolite • $CaBSiO_4OH$

Chemical group: Boro-silicate

Datolite is a boro-silicate with simple
composition and a pale color. It is related to
the gadolinite group of minerals, which are
characterized by their high concentrations of
rare earth elements; some cerium and
lanthanum can occur as impurities in datolite.
It occurs in small quantities in basic igneous
rocks, pegmatites, and in metamorphic rocks.
Found in Harz, in Germany, Arendal, in
Norway, Massachusetts and New Jersey.

FAMILY: TOURMALINE

Tourmaline • $(Na,Ca)(Li,Mg,Fe,Al)_3(Al,Fe)_6 B_3Si_6O_{27}(O,OH,F)_4$

Chemical group: Boro-silicate

ID FACT FILE

CRYSTAL SYSTEM:
Trigonal

COLOR:
Black, blue; all colors

WHERE:
Igneous, metamorphic

ABUNDANCE:
Rock-forming

FORM:
Elongated prismatic crystals; also radiating, granular

CLEAVAGE:
None

HARDNESS:
7–7.5

SG:
3–3.2

LUSTER:
Vitreous

TRANSPARENCY:
Transparent to opaque

TESTS:
Choncoidal, uneven fracture. White streak. Striated crystals, triangular cross sections

LOOKALIKES:
Apatite

Tourmaline is a boro-silicate with variable composition. It occurs in small quantities in acid igneous rocks like granite, and is locally abundant or rock-forming. It also occurs in small quantities in many metamorphic rocks, like gneiss and mica-schist; also in sedimentary placer deposits. *Schorl* is an iron-rich black or blue variety. *Elbaite* is lithium-rich tourmaline, often pink or green. *Dravite* is magnesium-rich, yellow or brown. *Rubellite* is the name for the rose-pink variety often used as a semiprecious gem.

FAMILY: BORATE

ID FACT FILE

CRYSTAL SYSTEM:
Monoclinic

COLOR:
White

WHERE:
Sedimentary,
salt lakes

ABUNDANCE:
Restricted

FORM:
Prismatic
crystals; also
massive

CLEAVAGE:
Good cleavage in
two directions

HARDNESS:
2–2.5

SG:
1.7

LUSTER:
Vitreous

TRANSPARENCY:
Translucent

TESTS:
White streak.
Tastes sweet or
alkaline (test not
recommended)

LOOKALIKES:
Colemanite and
other borate

Borax • $Na_2B_4O_7.10H_2O$

Chemical group: Borate

Borax is the best-known borate mineral and has a distinctive crystal form and low SG. It occurs in desiccated salt lakes, playas, or borax marshes together with other borates such as *colemanite*, as in California. Borates, including borax, may also form as hydrothermal deposits from volcanic hot springs.

FAMILY: FOSSIL RESIN

Amber •
$C_{10}H_{16}O$ (variable)

Chemical group: Succinic acid

ID FACT FILE

CRYSTAL SYSTEM:
Amorphous

COLOR:
Orangy yellow to brown

WHERE:
Sedimentary

ABUNDANCE:
Restricted

FORM:
Nodular

CLEAVAGE:
None

HARDNESS:
2–2.5

SG:
1.1–1.3

LUSTER:
Greasy, resinous

TRANSPARENCY:
Transparent to opaque

TESTS:
Conchoidal fracture. White streak

LOOKALIKES:
Unlikely to be mistaken

Amber is a fossil resin that is frequently clouded and can contain fossil insects or parts of plant debris; it is the fossilized resin from pine trees. It occurs in young sedimentary rocks of estuarine origin or beach deposits. Found in countries around the Baltic Sea, in Romania, and in Siberia.

FAMILY: LIGNITE COAL

ID FACT FILE

CRYSTAL SYSTEM:
Amorphous

COLOR:
Very black

WHERE:
Sedimentary

ABUNDANCE:
Restricted

FORM:
Nodular, even-colored lumps

CLEAVAGE:
None

HARDNESS:
1.5–2.5

SG:
1.2

LUSTER:
Brilliant, resinous

TRANSPARENCY:
Opaque

TESTS:
Conchoidal fracture. Brown to black streak. Takes a good polish

LOOKALIKES:
Coals

Jet • C,H,N,O (variable)

Chemical group: Carbon-rich

Jet is an intense black-colored variety of lignite or brown coal that takes a very high polish and is used for ornaments, as in Whitby, in Yorkshire, in northern England. Jet was also known to the Greeks from Asia Minor. Lignite occurs in coal-bearing sedimentary strata, and has a brilliant luster; often contains fossil plant remains. Found in England, Germany, and Hungary.

Andesite

Chemical group: Intermediate igneous

ID FACT FILE

ESSENTIAL MINERALS:
Plagioclase, augite

OTHER MINERALS:
Olivine, hornblende, biotite, quartz, magnetite, alkali feldspar, apatite

MINERAL PROPORTIONS:
Plagioclase> augite

COLOR:
Medium to pale gray, pinkish, greenish. Distinctive texture

TEXTURAL FEATURES:
Large crystals (phenocrysts) including plagioclase always present; set in finely crystalline or glassy matrix, which may have vesicles

DISTRIBUTION:
Related to subduction, island arcs, calderas

ABUNDANCE:
Widespread

LOOKALIKES:
Tephrite, dacite

Named for the Andes in South America, where it is abundant, andesite is intermediate in composition between basalt and rhyolite. The rock texture is characterized by two grain sizes (*porphyritic*); large crystals of plagioclase, sometimes angular and broken, and several mafic crystals are set in a "basaltic" or glassy matrix. The mafic minerals can include any or all of olivine, hornblende, biotite, and pyroxenes. It is the characteristic product of volcanoes related to subduction as around the Pacific rim.

FAMILY: GRANITE

ID FACT FILE

ESSENTIAL MINERALS:
Alkali feldspar,
plagioclase,
quartz

OTHER MINERALS:
Biotite,
hornblende,
muscovite,
biotite,
tourmaline,
apatite

MINERAL PROPORTIONS:
Alkali feldspar>
plagioclase>
quartz

COLOR:
Light-colored,
pinkish, reddish.
Distinctive
texture

TEXTURAL FEATURES:
Even-textured
rock, small
granular crystals,
sugary texture

DISTRIBUTION:
Related to large
granites

ABUNDANCE:
Widespread

LOOKALIKES:
Pelsite

Aplite

Chemical group: Acid igneous

Aplite is a fine-grained variety of granite with a granular sugary texture. It occurs as small bodies, dykes, or veins, associated with large masses of coarse-grained granite, or pegmatites, especially near the edges of large intrusions. Occasionally aplites can be found in rock types other than granite, such as syenite. A fine-grained granite with much less quartz and more feldspar called *felsite* can also occur.

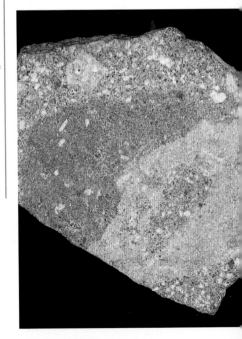

Basalt

Chemical group: Basic igneous

ID FACT FILE

ESSENTIAL MINERALS:
Plagioclase,
augite

OTHER MINERALS:
Olivine,
pyroxenes,
spinel, ilmenite,
magnetite,
apatite

MINERAL PROPORTIONS:
Plagioclase>
augite

COLOR:
Black, very dark
gray; paler and
greenish if
altered

TEXTURAL FEATURES:
Usually larger
crystals
(phenocrysts) set
in finely
crystalline
matrix, which
may have
vesicles and
occasionally
glass

DISTRIBUTION:
Oceanic islands,
continental
volcanoes, flood
plateau lavas

ABUNDANCE:
Widespread;
constitutes all
seafloor crust

LOOKALIKES:
Glassy volcanic
rocks

Basalt is a finely crystalline igneous rock, which is sometimes glassy, and represents rapidly cooled magma derived from the Earth's upper mantle. It is recognized primarily by its very dark color. It may contain visible larger crystals of olivine (olivine basalt; *see* p.164), pyroxene or plagioclase. It is the most widely distributed volcanic rock. Molten basaltic magma is very fluid and can form vast lava flows, as well as pillows. When cooled more slowly it forms dolerite or gabbro (*see* p.180 and p.183). Found in Antrim, in Ireland, Skye and Mull in Scotland, Iceland, Auvergne in France, in Germany, Italy and most countries.

FAMILY: BASALT

ID FACT FILE

ESSENTIAL MINERALS:
Plagioclase, augite, olivine

OTHER MINERALS:
Pyroxenes, spinel, ilmenite, magnetite, apatite

MINERAL PROPORTIONS:
Plagioclase> augite>olivine

COLOR:
Black, very dark gray; prominent green olivine crystals

TEXTURAL FEATURES:
Large olivine crystals (phenocrysts) set in finely crystalline matrix, which may have vesicles and occasionally glass

DISTRIBUTION:
Oceanic islands, continental volcanoes

ABUNDANCE:
Widespread

LOOKALIKES:
Unlikely to be mistaken

Olivine Basalt

Chemical group: Basic igneous

Olivine basalt is a variety of basalt (*see* p.163). Larger crystals of olivine are distinctive rounded or stubby prisms. Varieties particularly rich in olivine may be called *picrite*. Two further varieties which have large crystals of both green olivine and black augite, as well as abundant rounded holes after volcanic gas, are known as *oceanite* (with just a little augite) and *ankaramite* (with approximately equal amounts of olivine and augite).

Dacite

Chemical group: Intermediate igneous

Dacite is named after a province in Romania. It is intermediate to acidic in composition, between andesite and rhyolite. The rock texture is characterized by two grain sizes (porphyritic); large crystals of plagioclase and quartz, sometimes angular and broken, and mafic crystals are set in a "basaltic" or glassy matrix. The mafic minerals are pyroxene, hornblende, or biotite. Olivine absent, and more quartz than andesite.

ID FACT FILE

ESSENTIAL MINERALS:
Plagioclase, quartz, hornblende/biotite/pyroxene

OTHER MINERALS:
Alkali feldspar, magnetite, apatite

MINERAL PROPORTIONS:
Plagioclase>quartz

COLOR:
Pale gray, pinkish, greenish. Distinctive texture

TEXTURAL FEATURES:
Large crystals (phenocrysts) including plagioclase always present; set in finely crystalline or glassy matrix, which may have vesicles and often shows a good flow texture

DISTRIBUTION:
Related to subduction, island arcs, calderas

ABUNDANCE:
Widespread

LOOKALIKES:
Andesite

FAMILY: GRANITE/DACITE

ID FACT FILE

ESSENTIAL MINERALS:
Alkali feldspar,
plagioclase,
quartz

OTHER MINERALS:
Hornblende,
mica, pyroxene,
magnetite, glass,
kaolinite

**MINERAL
PROPORTIONS:**
Mostly alkali
feldspar

COLOR:
Pinkish, reddish,
brownish colored

TEXTURAL FEATURES:
Irregular volcanic
texture (see tuff;
p.175), glassy
shards, many
gas voids

DISTRIBUTION:
Occurs in vast
sheets
associated with
large calderas

ABUNDANCE:
Widespread

LOOKALIKES:
Tuff

Ignimbrite

Chemical group: Acid igneous

Ignimbrite is a silica-rich igneous rock
occurring in large sheet-like bodies which
partly resemble lava flows. It is formed from
violent eruptions of dacite or rhyolite magma
during catastrophic caldera collapse.
Ignimbrites represent products of the largest
known volcanic eruptions on Earth and may
extend over tens or even hundreds of miles.
They contain concentrations of pumice and
distinctive flamelike shattered glass fragments;
they show cooling joints like lavas. They are
associated with andesite, dacite, and rhyolite
volcanism, as in the Andes, in South America,
New Zealand, in Oregon and Montana, and
with Pacific rim volcanism; they also occur in
oceanic islands, as at Tenerife in the Canary
Islands. Older ignimbrites have infilled voids
and are harder, as in Snowdonia, in Wales and
in the Lake District in northern England.

ESSENTIAL MINERALS:
Olivine,
pyroxene, glass

OTHER MINERALS:
Plagioclase,
spinel,
serpentine,
amphibole,
chlorite

MINERAL PROPORTIONS:
Olivine or
pyroxene
dominant

COLOR:
Dark-colored,
greenish.
Distinctive
texture

TEXTURAL FEATURES:
Large elongated
feathery crystals
set in finely
crystalline,
feathery or
glassy matrix
(spinifex texture)

DISTRIBUTION:
Related to
metamorphic
"greenstone
belts" in very old
crust and rarely
in some younger
igneous flood
basalt provinces

ABUNDANCE:
Common

LOOKALIKES:
Texture unlikely
to be mistaken

Komatiite

Chemical group: Basic/ultrabasic igneous

Komatiites are rapidly-cooled volcanic lavas formed from volcanic eruptions of the hottest magmas known on Earth (perhaps 2730–2910°F/1500–1600°C). They are associated with substantial sulfide ore deposits for nickel and other metals, sometimes including gold and platinum. Found at Barberton in South Africa, Zimbabwe, Australia, Abitibi, Ontario, Canada, Finland, and India. The youngest komatiites (approximately 60 million years old) occur in Isla Gorgona, in Colombia.

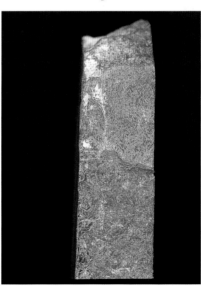

FAMILY: VOLCANIC

ID FACT FILE

ESSENTIAL MINERALS:
Glass

OTHER MINERALS:
Alkali feldspar,
quartz

**MINERAL
PROPORTIONS:**
Mostly glass

COLOR:
Black, dark
colors; some
white features

TEXTURAL FEATURES:
Massive glass
with conchoidal
fracture; thin
flakes
transparent

DISTRIBUTION:
Relatively young
volcanic

ABUNDANCE:
Locally common

LOOKALIKES:
Unlikely to be
mistaken

Obsidian

Chemical group: Intermediate/acid igneous

Obsidian is a silica-rich natural glass, associated
with young lava flows. It has a distinctive glassy
nature, with conchoidal fracture and very sharp
edges; its use for knives and arrows makes it an
important archeological material. Obsidian
occurs as crusts on lavas, as complete flows or as
near-surface volcanic domes. It is usually of
rhyolite composition and forms by slow flow of
very viscous lava; other obsidian compositions
include phonolite, andesite and trachyte. Found
in Iceland, in Anatolia in Turkey, Lipari in Italy,
in Hungary, in New Mexico and Wyoming, and
in Japan. *Pitchstone* is a resinous variety of
natural volcanic glass, developed by aging; it has
more crystals similar to rhyolite and occurs in
older volcanic and igneous rocks, as in Eigg and
Arran in Scotland, Saxony in Germany, Southern
Tyrol in Italy, and in the state of Colorado.

ID FACT FILE

ESSENTIAL MINERALS:
Alkali feldspar, nepheline, pyroxene

OTHER MINERALS:
Amphibole, melanite, olivine, magnetite, apatite, glass

MINERAL PROPORTIONS:
Feldspar> nepheline> pyroxene

COLOR:
Gray, greenish, brownish

TEXTURAL FEATURES:
Large crystals of feldspar and nepheline in a fine-grained matrix, which may be glassy

DISTRIBUTION:
Continental rifts, alkaline volcanism

ABUNDANCE:
Common

LOOKALIKES:
Basalt

Phonolite

Chemical group: Alkaline igneous

Phonolite is an alkaline igneous rock with characteristic blocky or tabular feldspar (sanidine/anorthoclase), squarish nepheline crystals, and black pyroxene (aegirine-augite). It is the fine-grained equivalent to nepheline syenite. It occurs primarily as lava flows but also as small subvolcanic bodies; thicker bodies show columnar jointing. Phonolites occur in huge quantities in some thick continental lava piles, as in the East African Rift Valley. Found in Kaiserstuhl in Germany, Auvergne in France, Devon in England, and in Montana.

ID FACT FILE

ESSENTIAL MINERALS:
Alkali feldspar,
plagioclase,
quartz

OTHER MINERALS:
Pyroxene,
amphibole,
zircon,
magnetite,
apatite

**MINERAL
PROPORTIONS:**
Mostly feldspars
and quartz

COLOR:
Pale gray,
reddish,
brownish; darker
when old

TEXTURAL FEATURES:
Fine-grained
rock, often
glassy with larger
quartz and
feldspar crystals

DISTRIBUTION:
Related to
subduction,
continental
volcanoes,
calderas

ABUNDANCE:
Common

LOOKALIKES:
Trachyte

Rhyolite

Chemical group: Acid igneous

Rhyolite is a fine-grained volcanic equivalent
to granite. It is the most silica-rich volcanic
rock (>66% SiO_2) and forms thick viscous
lobate lava flows and volcanic domes, at times
with columnar cooling joints. It often shows
prominent parallel banding with different
shades of color produced during flow. In young
volcanoes it is often glassy and may be vesicular;
older rhyolites are darker, due to staining from
iron minerals and alteration of glass. Found in
the Lake District in England, Snowdonia in
Wales, in Iceland, Vosges in France, Saxony in
Germany, Lipari and Tuscany in Italy, and in
the Andes of South America.

ID FACT FILE

ESSENTIAL MINERALS:
Feldspathoid,
pyroxene,
hornblende,
plagioclase,
alkali feldspar

OTHER MINERALS:
Olivine,
magnetite,
analcime, apatite

MINERAL PROPORTIONS:
Variable, but
similar amounts
of dark/light
minerals;
prominent
feldspathoids

COLOR:
Dark gray,
greenish,
brownish; mottled
appearance

TEXTURAL FEATURES:
Large crystals of
nepheline or
leucite with
pyroxene and
hornblende in a
basaltlike or
glassy matrix; gas
voids common

DISTRIBUTION:
Related to
alkaline
volcanism in
continental rifts
or oceanic
islands

ABUNDANCE:
Common

LOOKALIKES:
Basalt lacks
prominent
feldspathoids

Tephrite

Chemical group: Basic/alkaline igneous

Tephrite is a basaltlike lava but with
prominent feldspathoids, nepheline and/or
leucite, together with pyroxene (augite) and
hornblende in a fine-grained or glassy matrix.
Voids caused by volcanic gas may be lined
with zeolites. It occurs as lava flows associated
with relatively young alkaline volcanoes.
Found in Vesuvius in Italy, Auvergne in
France, Eifel and in Kaiserstuhl in Germany.
Basanite is a variety of tephrite that has
olivine and less feldspathoid and is more
similar to basalt; found in the Canary Islands,
in Eifel in Germany, Ayrshire in Scotland.
Limburgite is a variety with mostly glass.

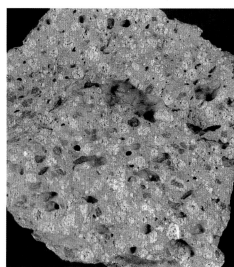

ID FACT FILE

ESSENTIAL MINERALS:
Alkali feldspar,
nepheline or
quartz

OTHER MINERALS:
Pyroxene,
amphibole,
melanite,
magnetite,
apatite

MINERAL PROPORTIONS:
Mostly alkali
feldspar.
Feldspar>
nepheline>
pyroxene

COLOR:
Pale gray,
pinkish, brownish

TEXTURAL FEATURES:
Fine-grained rock
with few dark
crystals

DISTRIBUTION:
Continental rifts,
alkaline
volcanism

ABUNDANCE:
Common

LOOKALIKES:
Phonolite,
rhyolite

Trachyte

Chemical group: Alkaline igneous

Trachyte is a fine-grained, pale-colored, alkaline igneous rock, made mostly of alkali feldspar (sanidine/anorthoclase). It is the fine-grained equivalent of plutonic syenite. It occurs primarily as lava flows but also as small subvolcanic bodies; thicker bodies show columnar jointing. It often occurs in association with phonolites as in the East African Rift Valley. Found in Devon, in England, Westerwald in Germany, North Wales, Auvergne in France, and in Colorado.

Pillow lava

Chemical group: Basic igneous

Volcanic pillows form when lava flows, usually basaltic, enter water, as at submarine eruptions along ocean ridges forming a continuous layer of all seafloors, and locally at oceanic islands, e.g. Hawaii, Iceland, and the Canary Islands. The rapid chilling produces a glassy margin, radial cooling joints, and concentric distribution of gas voids concentrated toward the rim. Pillows are head-sized to pillow-sized and have rounded shapes, often with downward-pointing tongues between successively accumulated pillows. The gas voids frequently become filled with secondary minerals such as zeolites and calcite. Old pillows are commonly found in uplifted relics of seafloor (ophiolite), as in the Southern Uplands in Scotland and in Cyprus.

ID FACT FILE

ESSENTIAL MINERALS:
Basaltic minerals plus glass (or altered glass)

OTHER MINERALS:
None

MINERAL PROPORTIONS:
Similar to basalt; glass often replaced by chlorite/clays

COLOR:
Black; dark gray, reddish or greenish when old

TEXTURAL FEATURES:
Characteristic shapes, gas voids, radial cooling joints, external glassy margin

DISTRIBUTION:
Basaltic lavas which flow into water; oceanic islands, seafloor

ABUNDANCE:
Abundant

LOOKALIKES:
Unlikely to be mistaken

FAMILY: VOLCANIC DEPOSITS

ID FACT FILE

ESSENTIAL MINERALS:
Mostly glass

OTHER MINERALS:
None

MINERAL PROPORTIONS:
Very few if any minerals

COLOR:
Pale gray, cream, white, greenish

TEXTURAL FEATURES:
Frothy texture of gas voids and glass, sometimes lacy

DISTRIBUTION:
Generally restricted to silica-rich volcanoes

ABUNDANCE:
Common

LOOKALIKES:
Unlikely to be mistaken

Pumice

Chemical group: Intermediate/acid igneous

Pumice is formed quickly as a mixture of expanding volcanic gas and magma. The resulting frothy texture superficially resembles a sponge, but the pores are not connected; hence pumice floats on water. It occurs in silica-rich volcanoes during violent eruptions of gas-rich magma, like dacite and rhyolite. The glass alters to clay minerals, producing the whitish colors and rather soft pumice. Occurs with bedded tuffs or ignimbrites, as in Santorini in Greece, Lipari and Naples in Italy, Iceland, Auvergne in France, Canary Islands, and the Andes of South America. *Scoria* is less frothy, denser glass that occurs in basaltic or alkaline volcanoes and is usually reddish.

ID FACT FILE

ESSENTIAL MINERALS:
Any rock-forming minerals

OTHER MINERALS:
Glass, old rock fragments

MINERAL PROPORTIONS:
Any

COLOR:
Brown, gray, yellow, red

TEXTURAL FEATURES:
Bedded, porous, loose, uncemented; highly variable

DISTRIBUTION:
All young volcanoes; especially andesites and acid igneous varieties

ABUNDANCE:
Abundant

LOOKALIKES:
Uncemented sediments

Tuff

Chemical group: All igneous

Volcanic tuff is the general term for all uncemented or loose deposits of volcanoes, also known as pyroclastic rocks. These grade into genuine sedimentary rocks. The composition reflects the general parent magma and igneous rock type of the source volcano. Tuffs are subdivided according to grain size; *ash* is the finest (<2 mm), *lapilli* are small pea-sized pebbles (2–64 mm), and *blocks* and *bombs* are the largest (>64 mm, commonly up to yard-scale sizes). Coarse materials are only found close to the volcano, while finer materials are more widely dispersed. Blocks are usually solidified magma broken from vents, lavas, or domes. Volcanic bombs are formed from hot lava blobs that are chilled during passage through the air (*see* p.176). Cemented or heat-welded varieties of tuff include ignimbrite (*see* p.166).

FAMILY: VOLCANIC DEPOSITS

ID FACT FILE

ESSENTIAL MINERALS:
Any rock-forming minerals plus glass

OTHER MINERALS:
None

MINERAL PROPORTIONS:
Similar to the parent magma

COLOR:
Reddish; black or gray when fresh

TEXTURAL FEATURES:
Characteristic shapes, gas voids

DISTRIBUTION:
Many young volcanoes; especially basic, intermediate and alkaline varieties

ABUNDANCE:
Abundant

LOOKALIKES:
Unlikely to be mistaken

Volcanic bomb

Chemical group: Most igneous

Volcanic bombs are distinctive forms of solidified lava, usually with crystals, formed from ejected blobs of hot lava which rapidly cool when thrown through the air. They tend to rotate during flight, resulting in twisted, spindlelike, or contorted shapes. Usually solid before impact, they sometimes bend, and some are modified by rolling down slopes; gas-rich lava bombs may continue to expand slightly resulting in *breadcrust* forms. Often black and glassy when freshly formed, they rapidly change to a reddish color due to iron oxides. Found in Vesuvius, Etna, and Stromboli in Italy, in Iceland, the Canary Islands, the Massif Central in France, and in the state of Hawaii.

FAMILY: GABBRO

ID FACT FILE

ESSENTIAL MINERALS:
Plagioclase

OTHER MINERALS:
Pyroxenes,
olivine, spinel,
ilmenite,
magnetite,
biotite, apatite

MINERAL PROPORTIONS:
Plagioclase
makes up >90%

COLOR:
White, pale gray

TEXTURAL FEATURES:
Granitic texture,
crystals
intergrown; may
show alignment
of platy feldspars
or layering

DISTRIBUTION:
Deeper
continental crust
e.g. Norway,
Labrador and
Quebec (Canada),
South Africa

ABUNDANCE:
Locally abundant
but much less
common than
gabbro

LOOKALIKES:
Unlikely to be
mistaken

Anorthosite

Chemical group: Ultrabasic igneous

Anorthosite is a very plagioclase-rich variety of
the gabbro family. The plagioclase is almost
pure anorthite in composition, giving the rock
a low silica content and ultrabasic composition
(SiO_2 < wt.%). The dark minerals, which are
chiefly pyroxenes, olivine, and spinel, make up
less than 10 percent of the rock. It occurs as
discrete layers in some large ultrabasic
intrusions, as in Rhum and Skye in Scotland.
The photograph illustrates half-inch-scale
bands of pure anorthosite alternating with thin
dark layers richer in pyroxene and olivine: a
layered anorthosite. Smashed anorthosite
(breccia) forms the highly reflective bright
surface of parts of the Moon.

ID FACT FILE

ESSENTIAL MINERALS:
Calcite, dolomite

OTHER MINERALS:
Forsterite, diopside, mica, magnetite, siderite, apatite, melanite, melilite, barite, pyrochlore, and rare minerals

MINERAL PROPORTIONS:
Mostly carbonates

COLOR:
White, pale-colored

TEXTURAL FEATURES:
Coarse-grained interlocking carbonate crystals, few dark minerals

DISTRIBUTION:
Occurs in large igneous masses and as volcanic rocks

ABUNDANCE:
Restricted

LOOKALIKES:
Marble

Carbonatite

Chemical group: Alkaline igneous

Carbonatite is a rare but distinctive rock whose carbonate minerals "fizz" with dilute acid. It occurs in association with alkaline igneous rocks, such as plutonic nepheline syenite and ijolite and volcanic nephelinite and melilitite. Currently only one volcano erupts carbonatite magma: Oldoinyo Lengai in Tanzania. Carbonatites are found in continental rifts or grabens as in East Africa, Kaiserstuhl in Germany and Oslo in Norway. Old carbonatites are mined for niobium, tantalum and rare earth minerals, as in Finland, Brazil, South Africa, and Kola in Russia.

FAMILY: DIORITE

ID FACT FILE

ESSENTIAL MINERALS:
Plagioclase, hornblende, biotite

OTHER MINERALS:
Quartz, augite, magnetite, alkali feldspar, apatite, chlorite

MINERAL PROPORTIONS:
Mostly plagioclase

COLOR:
Light to dark gray, greenish

TEXTURAL FEATURES:
Medium- to fine-grained with interlocking crystals, sometimes porphyritic with scattered larger crystals

DISTRIBUTION:
Occurs in small intrusive igneous bodies, sometimes near the edges of granites

ABUNDANCE:
Locally common

LOOKALIKES:
Gabbro, dolerite

Diorite

Chemical group: Intermediate igneous

Diorite is a fine- to medium-grained completely crystalline igneous rock with no glass and no void spaces. It is used as ornamental material since it polishes well. Darker varieties contain more hornblende, augite, or biotite and can appear very similar to gabbro or dolerite, though the presence of some biotite is usually diagnostic. Altered varieties often contain chlorite. Found in Argyll in Scotland, Jersey in the Channel Islands, Harz in Germany, in Finland, and in the state of Washington. Varieties with golf-ball sized round "bull's eyes" of minerals are known as orbicular diorites, as in Corsica in France and in Finland. Below: microscopic view of thin section.

FAMILY: BASALT

ID FACT FILE

ESSENTIAL MINERALS:
Plagioclase,
augite

OTHER MINERALS:
Olivine,
hornblende,
biotite, quartz,
magnetite,
ilmenite, alkali
feldspar, apatite

MINERAL PROPORTIONS:
Plagioclase>
augite

COLOR:
Dark medium
gray. Distinctive
texture

TEXTURAL FEATURES:
Medium-grained
variety of basalt,
with easily
distinguished
"spiky" white
plagioclase set
in dark mineral
matrix, mostly
pyroxene; entirely
crystalline, no
glass but may
have vesicles

DISTRIBUTION:
Common variety
of subvolcanic
basalt, in minor
intrusions like
dykes and sills

ABUNDANCE:
Widespread

LOOKALIKES:
Basalt, gabbro

Dolerite

Chemical group: Basic igneous

Dolerite is the medium-grained variety of
basalt that is not as coarse-grained as gabbro. It
typically occurs as dykes and sills, as in the
Whin sill in the north of England, which
displays prominent columnar cooling joints. In
addition to pyroxene (augite), dolerite may
contain some olivine or quartz (not both) and a
variety of less abundant minerals. When
altered, it often takes a greenish color due to
the presence of chlorite minerals. The texture
observable with a hand lens shows small white
plagioclases surrounded by larger dark augite,
with random orientation.

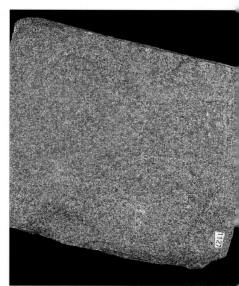

FAMILY: PERIDOTITE

ID FACT FILE

ESSENTIAL MINERALS:
Olivine

OTHER MINERALS:
Chromite,
pyroxene, mica

MINERAL PROPORTIONS:
More than 90%
olivine

COLOR:
Green when
fresh

TEXTURAL FEATURES:
Distinctive
olivine, granular

DISTRIBUTION:
Occurs in uplifted
mantle rocks, in
large basic
intrusions

ABUNDANCE:
Restricted

LOOKALIKES:
Peridotite

Dunite

Chemical group: Ultrabasic igneous

Dunite is a rock made up almost entirely of one
mineral, olivine (forsterite). It reflects the color
of olivine. When altered, it can be replaced by
serpentine, which may be reddish. It occurs
in large masses of metamorphosed olivine-rich
rocks like peridotite and serpentinite; it also
occurs in association with other ultramafic
igneous rocks, such as plutonic pyroxenite
and volcanic komatiite. Found in Aheim, in
Norway, Troödos in Cyprus, Mount Dun
in New Zealand, and in South Africa.

FAMILY: GABBRO

ID FACT FILE

ESSENTIAL MINERALS:
Plagioclase,
pyroxene,
hornblende

OTHER MINERALS:
Biotite,
feldspathoids,
ilmenite,
magnetite,
apatite, titanite

MINERAL PROPORTIONS:
Similar amounts
of light
(feldspars) and
dark minerals

COLOR:
Dark gray;
mottled

TEXTURAL FEATURES:
Granitic texture,
crystals
intergrown;
sometimes
porphyritic

DISTRIBUTION:
Continental
crust, associated
with alkaline
igneous rocks

ABUNDANCE:
Uncommon

LOOKALIKES:
Gabbro

Essexite

Chemical group: Basic igneous

Essexite is a variety of gabbro with a higher
total content of dark minerals, including
titanium-bearing pyroxene and hornblende. It
often includes small amounts of feldspathoids,
such as nepheline and analcime. Its texture is
medium- to coarse-grained as for gabbro (*see*
p.183). It forms only small bodies, as in
Southern Tyrol, in Italy, on the east coast of
Scotland and in Kaiserstuhl, Germany. A
variety of gabbro similar to essexite but with
more nepheline is *theralite*, as found in
Scotland and in Auvergne, France.

ID FACT FILE

Gabbro

Chemical group: Basic igneous

ESSENTIAL MINERALS:
Plagioclase,
pyroxenes

OTHER MINERALS:
Olivine,
hornblende,
spinel, ilmenite,
magnetite,
apatite

MINERAL PROPORTIONS:
Plagioclase>
augite

COLOR:
Dark gray,
greenish,
brownish

TEXTURAL FEATURES:
Granitic texture,
crystals
intergrown; may
show alignment
of platy
feldspars, or
layering

DISTRIBUTION:
Deeper
continental crust;
uplifted oceanic
crust

ABUNDANCE:
Widespread

LOOKALIKES:
Dolerite, diorite

Gabbro is the coarsely crystalline equivalent of basalt, and results from complete slow crystallization at depth in the crust. It is a dark-colored rock, with strongly intergrown minerals, making it tough. The major dark minerals are pyroxene, olivine, and hornblende. The pyroxene can include both augite and enstatite-hypersthene. The plagioclase is close to anorthite in composition. Varieties of gabbro include olivine-rich *troctolite* (*see* p.197), hypersthene-rich *norite* (*see* p.192), and nearly pure plagioclase rock called *anorthosite* (*see* p.177).

ID FACT FILE

ESSENTIAL MINERALS:
Alkali feldspar,
plagioclase,
quartz

OTHER MINERALS:
Biotite,
hornblende,
augite,
muscovite,
apatite, zircon,
magnetite

MINERAL PROPORTIONS:
Alkali feldspar>
plagioclase>
quartz. These 3
minerals make
up more than
80% of the rock

COLOR:
Mottled, gray,
pink, or yellowish

TEXTURAL FEATURES:
Coarse-grained
interlocking
crystals;
granular. Quartz
forms irregular
shapes between
feldspars (but
see Varieties,
opposite)

DISTRIBUTION:
Continental crust
of all ages

ABUNDANCE:
Widespread,
plutons

LOOKALIKES:
Granodiorite,
diorite

Granite

Chemical group: Acid igneous

Granite and other rocks of the granite family are the most widely distributed of the deeper (plutonic) igneous rocks; they are a major component of the Earth's crust. Alkali feldspar is the dominant mineral and can form larger crystals; its color determines the color of the rock. Hard and tough, it is used in construction and monuments. Characteristic weathering can lead to rounded topography, relic stacks of granite slabs called "tors," as in southwestern England, and onion-skin exfoliation of massive boulders, as in South Africa.

ID FACT FILE

ESSENTIAL MINERALS:
Alkali feldspar,
plagioclase,
quartz

OTHER MINERALS:
Biotite,
hornblende,
augite,
muscovite,
apatite, zircon,
magnetite

**MINERAL
PROPORTIONS:**
Alkali feldspar>
plagioclase>
quartz. These 3
minerals make
up more than
80% of the rock

COLOR:
Mottled, gray,
pink, or yellowish

TEXTURAL FEATURES:
Coarse-grained
interlocking
crystals;
granular, or other
textures (*see*
main text)

DISTRIBUTION:
Continental crust
of all ages

ABUNDANCE:
Widespread,
plutons

LOOKALIKES:
Granodiomte
diorite

Above:
Graphic granite

Below:
Detail of biotite
granite

Granite Varieties

Chemical group: Acid igneous

Graphic granite (illustrated) occurs in
pegmatite, and has quartz which resembles
Egyptian writing. *Biotite granite* and
tourmaline granite have up to 20 percent of
these minerals. *Orbicular granite* is rare; it has
orange-sized circular spheres of pale granite
within normal granite. *Rapakivi granite* has
golfball-sized spheres of pinkish feldspar
surrounded by a matrix of darker granite.
Porphyry is a granite with two distinct sizes of
crystals (porphyritic texture) that tends to
occur in small bodies.

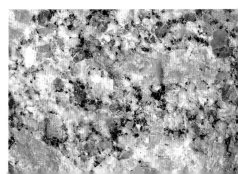

FAMILY: GRANITE

ID FACT FILE

ESSENTIAL MINERALS:
Plagioclase, alkali feldspar, quartz

OTHER MINERALS:
Biotite, hornblende, muscovite, augite, apatite, zircon, magnetite

MINERAL PROPORTIONS:
Plagioclase>alkali feldspar>quartz. These three minerals make up more than 60% of the rock

COLOR:
Mottled gray, dark gray

TEXTURAL FEATURES:
Coarse-grained interlocking crystals; granular. Quartz forms irregular shapes between feldspars. Similar to granite

DISTRIBUTION:
Continental crust of all ages

ABUNDANCE:
Widespread, small plutons

LOOKALIKES:
Granite, diorite

Granodiorite

Chemical group: Acid igneous

Granodiorite is similar to granite, except that plagioclase feldspar is more abundant than alkali feldspar, and the rock contains more dark minerals. It is a darker-colored rock and less abundant than granite generally. Most of the rock is made of feldspars and quartz or "felsic" minerals. A hand lens should reveal the identity of the mafic minerals, biotite, and hornblende; quartz is often vitreous dull gray compared to white or pale gray feldspar. Found in Southern Uplands in Scotland, in southern Norway, in Germany, and in Austria.

FAMILY: QUARTZOLITE

ID FACT FILE

ESSENTIAL MINERALS:
Quartz

OTHER MINERALS:
Mica, feldspars, topaz, fluorite, apatite, tourmaline

MINERAL PROPORTIONS:
Quartz>60%

COLOR:
Pale gray, reddish

TEXTURAL FEATURES:
Coarse-grained interlocking crystals; granular, often with cavities

DISTRIBUTION:
Continental crust

ABUNDANCE:
Restricted to bodies or veins a few hundred yards in size

LOOKALIKES:
Pegmatite

Greisen

Chemical group: Acid igneous

Greisen is a rock made mostly of quartz. It is usually associated with granites and may form when feldspar is removed by hydrothermal fluids long after the granite solidified. Generally light gray or stained brownish by iron. Well formed, and therefore collectable, accessory minerals are often found concentrated in patches and cavities, and can include gem material, such as topaz, as in Brazil. Occasionally host to tungsten, tin, or molybdenum minerals, as in Cornwall and Devon and in England.

FAMILY: FOIDOLITE

ID FACT FILE

ESSENTIAL MINERALS:
Nepheline,
pyroxene

OTHER MINERALS:
Amphibole, mica,
titanite,
magnetite,
calcite

MINERAL PROPORTIONS:
Nepheline>
pyroxene

COLOR:
Dark-colored

TEXTURAL FEATURES:
Coarse-grained,
squarish
nepheline,
prismatic
pyroxene, or
interlocking

DISTRIBUTION:
Occurs in small
bodies within or
adjacent to large
igneous masses
of syenites or
with alkaline
volcanoes

ABUNDANCE:
Rare

LOOKALIKES:
Pyroxenite

Ijolite

Chemical group: Alkaline igneous

Ijolite is mainly composed of just two minerals,
nepheline and pyroxene (aegirine-augite or
aegirine). Nepheline forms square-shaped
crystals set among black pyroxene. It occurs as
small bodies in association with alkaline igneous
rocks like nepheline syenite, and with alkaline
volcanic rocks like phonolite, nephelinite, and
carbonatite. Relatively young ijolites are found
in the East African Rift Valley. Older ijolites are
found in Norway, Sweden, Finland, Kola in
Russia, and in Brazil. The photograph shows a
variety with very large pyroxene.

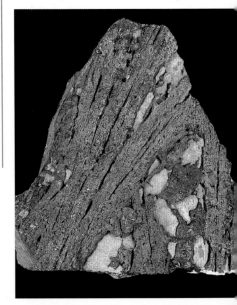

Kimberlite

Chemical group: Alkaline igneous

Kimberlite is an olivine-rich rock, with a distinctive porphyritic texture (having minerals of two sizes). The olivine is often altered to serpentine. It is often characterized by its minor minerals, which include red pyrope, brown phlogopite, and apple-green diopside. It is also famous for hosting diamonds. It forms vertical pipelike bodies with tops shaped like ice-cream cones called diatremes, and also dykes and sills. Found in Kimberley, in South Africa, Zaire, Tanzania, India, Siberia in Russia, in Brazil, and in Canada. The photograph is of octahedral diamond in kimberlite.

Lamprophyre

Chemical group: Intermediate igneous

ID FACT FILE

ESSENTIAL MINERALS:
Augite, mica, hornblende, plagioclase, orthoclase

OTHER MINERALS:
Olivine or quartz, magnetite, apatite

MINERAL PROPORTIONS:
Mostly dark minerals

COLOR:
Dark-colored

TEXTURAL FEATURES:
Larger dark-colored crystals (phenocrysts) set in finely crystalline or glassy matrix of feldspar

DISTRIBUTION:
Peripheral to large plutons or subvolcanic

ABUNDANCE:
Common

LOOKALIKES:
Basalt, dolerite

Lamprophyre is a general name for fine-grained dark igneous rock with two sizes of crystals (porphyritic texture) but no large crystals of feldspar; compare with andesite (*see* p.161), which is the opposite. Its color reflects the high proportions of dark minerals, which can vary greatly. It usually forms small bodies, such as dykes, sometimes at the edge of larger intrusions. *Minette* is a mica-rich variety related to syenite. Found in Southern Uplands in Scotland, Devon in England, Oberpfalz, in Bavaria, Germany, and Vosges in France.

FAMILY: SYENITE

ID FACT FILE

ESSENTIAL MINERALS:
Alkali feldspar, plagioclase, augite, biotite

OTHER MINERALS:
Hornblende, magnetite, apatite, zircon, titanite, nepheline or quartz

MINERAL PROPORTIONS:
Alkali feldspar dominant

COLOR:
Dark gray, greenish, bluish. Distinctive internal peacock colors in large feldspar crystals

TEXTURAL FEATURES:
Coarse-grained rock with larger crystals of feldspar, and small clots of dark minerals

DISTRIBUTION:
Related to alkaline volcanism and continental rifting

ABUNDANCE:
Restricted

LOOKALIKES:
Unlikely to be mistaken

Larvikite

Chemical group: Alkaline igneous

Larvikite is a well known variety of syenite, valued for decorative purposes; polishing enhances the play of peacock colors in the feldspar (a variety of alkali feldspar but similar in appearance to labradorite; *see* plagioclase, p.93). The texture shows large feldspar crystals and small clots of dark minerals, which include biotite and other minerals. Larvikite occurs in large igneous plutonic bodies related to an old (Permian age) volcanic rift around Larvik near Oslo, in Norway. It is from this site that the rock takes its name.

FAMILY: GABBRO

ID FACT FILE

ESSENTIAL MINERALS:
Plagioclase,
hypersthene,
augite

OTHER MINERALS:
Olivine,
hornblende,
spinel, ilmenite,
magnetite,
apatite

MINERAL PROPORTIONS:
Plagioclase>
pyroxene

COLOR:
Dark gray,
greenish,
brownish

TEXTURAL FEATURES:
Granitic texture,
crystals
intergrown; may
show alignment
of platy
feldspars, or
layering

DISTRIBUTION:
Deeper
continental crust;
uplifted oceanic
crust

ABUNDANCE:
Common

LOOKALIKES:
Gabbro

Norite

Chemical group: Basic igneous

Norite is a variety of gabbro (*see* p.183), characterized by the dominance of hypersthene as the dark-colored mineral in the rock. Often difficult to distinguish, unless the bronzy luster of cleaved surfaces of hypersthene is visible. The famous nickel sulfide deposit in Sudbury, in Ontario, Canada, is associated with a large body of norite.

ID FACT FILE

ESSENTIAL MINERALS:
Alkali feldspar and either quartz or feldspathoid

OTHER MINERALS:
Variable e.g. albite, tourmaline, topaz, beryl, mica, apatite, zircon, titanite, and rare minerals

MINERAL PROPORTIONS:
Distinctive texture

COLOR:
Pale colored

TEXTURAL FEATURES:
Very large crystals, often perfectly formed; giant crystals are known

DISTRIBUTION:
Occurs in small bodies within or adjacent to large igneous masses of granites and syenites

ABUNDANCE:
Widespread

LOOKALIKES:
None

Pegmatite

Chemical group: Acid or alkaline igneous

Pegmatite is purely a textural term for the coarsest grain size of igneous rocks. Distinctive large crystals (half-inch-scale) may be perfectly formed, sometimes protruding into voids. The alkali feldspar can be orthoclase, or microcline and albite (plagioclase) may also occur. Pegmatites are the main source of many gem minerals, such as pink and green tourmaline and spodumene found in granite pegmatites from California and Brazil, and aquamarine and emerald from Colombia. Tin, copper, tungsten, and other metal mineralization is often associated with granite pegmatites, as in Cornwall, in England. Pegmatites associated with nepheline syenites often contain nepheline, zircon, titanite, and rare earth element minerals, as in Oslo, in Norway.

ID FACT FILE

ESSENTIAL MINERALS:
Alkali feldspar, plagioclase, nepheline, or quartz

OTHER MINERALS:
Pyroxene, biotite, amphibole, magnetite, apatite, zircon, titanite

MINERAL PROPORTIONS:
Alkali feldspar>plagioclase>less mafic minerals

COLOR:
Light to dark gray, reddish, brownish

TEXTURAL FEATURES:
Medium- to coarse-grained rock with larger crystals of feldspar and small clots of dark minerals

DISTRIBUTION:
Related to old alkaline volcanism and continental rifting

ABUNDANCE:
Restricted

LOOKALIKES:
Granite has much more quartz

Syenite

Chemical group: Alkaline igneous

Syenite is a feldspar-rich coarse-grained rock that is similar in many respects to granite, but has little or no quartz; instead of quartz it often contains the feldspathoid nepheline. The pyroxene is alkali-rich aegirine or aegirine-augite. Found in Borrolan in Scotland, in Saxony, in Germany, Oslo in Norway, in southern Portugal, Kola in Russia, Piedmonte in Italy, and Transvaal in South Africa.

There are several varieties of syenite. Nepheline syenite (*foyaite*) contains substantial nepheline and often has tabular feldspars, as in southern Portugal; it may also contain sodalite. *Monzonite* contains about equal proportions of orthoclase and plagioclase, as in South Tyrol in Italy. *Larvikite* is another variety (*see* p.191).

Syenite Varieties

Chemical group: Alkaline igneous

Nepheline syenite (foyaite)

Monzonite

FAMILY: GRANITE

ID FACT FILE

ESSENTIAL MINERALS:
Plagioclase, quartz, biotite, hornblende

OTHER MINERALS:
Alkali feldspar, muscovite, augite, apatite, zircon, magnetite

MINERAL PROPORTIONS:
Plagioclase> alkali feldspar> quartz. These three minerals make up more than 60% of the rock

COLOR:
Dark gray, mottled

TEXTURAL FEATURES:
Coarse-grained interlocking crystals; granular. Similar to granite. Dark minerals may be slightly larger

DISTRIBUTION:
Continental crust of all ages

ABUNDANCE:
Common, small plutons

LOOKALIKES:
Granite, granodiorite

Tonalite

Chemical group: Intermediate igneous

Tonalite is a variety of granodiorite with almost no alkali feldspar. The color reflects the color of plagioclase (gray) and is darker. Hornblende and biotite can occur as larger crystals in a pale matrix, giving a characteristic spotted appearance, as in Tonale district of South Tyrol, in Italy, southern Norway, Finland, and in Sweden. The variety *trondhjemite* is similar to tonalite but has higher quartz content and less dark minerals (<15 percent).

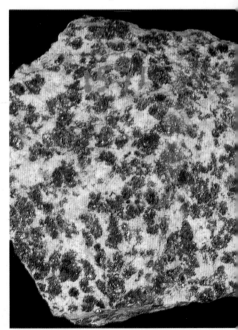

ID FACT FILE

ESSENTIAL MINERALS:
Plagioclase,
olivine

OTHER MINERALS:
Pyroxenes,
spinel,
magnetite,
apatite

MINERAL PROPORTIONS:
Plagioclase>
olivine

COLOR:
Dark gray,
greenish,
brownish

TEXTURAL FEATURES:
Granitic texture,
crystals
intergrown with
clots of dark
minerals

DISTRIBUTION:
Continental crust

ABUNDANCE:
Common

LOOKALIKES:
Gabbro,
anorthosite

Troctolite

Chemical group: Basic igneous

Troctolite, also known as trout stone, is a variety of gabbro (*see* p.183). It is characterized by its generally pale color and its spotted appearance, which is formed by clots of dark minerals; olivine is the chief mafic mineral. Where fresh, olivine in the rock is green, but where altered, olivine is frequently replaced by serpentine minerals, giving the rock a reddish or brownish color. It occurs with other gabbros in larger intrusive complexes as in Ardnamurchan, in Scotland.

ID FACT FILE

TYPICAL MINERALS:
Hornblende,
plagioclase

OTHER MINERALS:
Quartz, biotite,
chlorite, garnet,
epidote, zoisite

MINERAL PROPORTIONS:
Abundant
amphibole

GRAIN SIZE:
Fine to coarse-
grained, even-
textured;
massive or
schistlike

COLOR:
Dark gray,
greenish, black

TEXTURAL FEATURES:
Even-textured
rock, elongated
amphibole
crystals
sometimes
aligned

FOLIATION:
Usually poor;
occasionally
distinctive and
schistlike

CONDITIONS:
Low–moderate
pressure,
moderate–high
temperature

DISTRIBUTION:
Widespread

LOOKALIKES:
Basalt/gabbro

Amphibolite

Chemical group: Basic/intermediate

Amphibolite is a medium-grade metamorphic
rock. As well as hornblende and sodium-
calcium-rich plagioclase, it often has quartz or
garnet, as in *garnet amphibolite*. Amphibolite is
the hydrous product of metamorphism of basic
igneous rocks like gabbro and dolerite. It can
form massive bodies, and retain recognizable
basaltlike intrusive forms like dykes. Found in
the Grampian Mountains and in the northwest
of Scotland, in Donegal and Connemara in
Ireland, Hohe Tauern in Austria, St. Gotthard
in Switzerland, Baden and Bavaria in Germany,
and in Scandinavia.

Blueschist

Chemical group: Basic/intermediate

TYPICAL MINERALS:
Essential blue amphibole (glaucophane)

OTHER MINERALS:
Epidote, albite, calcite, garnet, quartz, zoisite, jadeite, mica, talc

MINERAL PROPORTIONS:
Plentiful glaucophane, others variable

GRAIN SIZE:
Fine- to medium-grained

COLOR:
Dark bluish gray

TEXTURAL FEATURES:
Parallel fabric of glaucophane forms planes of weakness; rock cleaves into thin platy pieces

FOLIATION:
Strong, parallel to platy minerals; often wavy

CONDITIONS:
High pressure, low temperature

DISTRIBUTION:
Rare but characteristic of old subducted oceanic crust; ophiolites

LOOKALIKES:
Unlikely to be mistaken

Blueschist is the highest pressure variety of schist that forms at rather low temperatures from old subducted oceanic crust. The bluish color is quite distinctive, often associated with minor yellowish-green epidote and minor garnet. Found in southern Brittany, in France, in Anglesey in Wales, in Tuscany in Italy, in Spitzbergen in Norway ,the Channel Islands, the Western Alps, California, and Cyprus.

FAMILY: ECLOGITE

ID FACT FILE

TYPICAL MINERALS:
Pyroxene, garnet

OTHER MINERALS:
Amphibole, kyanite, rutile, zoisite, plagioclase, quartz

MINERAL PROPORTIONS:
Garnet and pyroxene in similar amounts

GRAIN SIZE:
Medium, coarse

COLOR:
Gray, greenish, reddish

TEXTURAL FEATURES:
Prominent rounded garnets in a matrix of pyroxene crystals

FOLIATION:
Weak to moderate; often massive unfoliated

CONDITIONS:
Very high pressure, high temperature

DISTRIBUTION:
Rare, small bodies in high-grade terrains

LOOKALIKES:
Garnet amphibolite

Eclogite

Chemical group: Basic/ultrabasic

Eclogite is a dark-colored granular rock with distinctive reddish or orangy garnet (pyrope, almandine) set in a matrix of greenish pyroxene (omphacite). Other minerals are present in only minor amounts. It forms by high-grade metamorphism of basic igneous rocks like basalt, and is one of the products of subducted oceanic crust. It has the highest density (3.2–3.6) of silicate rocks in the crust. It occurs in Glenelg in Scotland, Hohe Tauern in Austria, Schwarzwald and Fichtelberg in Germany, and in California. It also occurs as xenoliths in kimberlite (*see* p.189) transported from the mantle. It is distinguished from amphibolite by its paler color.

ID FACT FILE

TYPICAL MINERALS:
Alkali feldspar, plagioclase, quartz, biotite

OTHER MINERALS:
Hornblende, garnet, cordierite, muscovite, sillimanite

MINERAL PROPORTIONS:
Alkali feldspar always present

GRAIN SIZE:
Coarse; variable across outcrop

COLOR:
Often banded dark and light; gray, reddish, brownish, greenish

TEXTURAL FEATURES:
Prominent, discontinuous banding due to repeated variation in proportions of dark and light minerals

FOLIATION:
Weak to distinct, parallel to dark mica-rich bands

CONDITIONS:
High pressure, moderate–high temperature

DISTRIBUTION:
Widespread

LOOKALIKES:
Migmatite, schist

Gneiss

Chemical group: Intermediate/acid

Gneiss is perhaps the commonest regional metamorphic rock type. Coarse-grained and often granitelike in composition, with abundant feldspars and quartz separated by bands of dark minerals, it is usually rich in biotite. Strong preferred orientation of the biotite leads to a preferred breaking direction. Named according to characteristic mineral (garnet-gneiss, cordierite-gneiss, etc.) or textural features, it includes *augen gneiss*, which has distinctive eye-shaped large alkali feldspar crystals. Occurs in northwestern Scotland, Central Alps, Massif Central, and Brittany in France, in Norway, in Sweden, Finland, in the Bavarian Woods in Germany, and in the Canadian Shield.

FAMILY: GRANULITE

Granulite

Chemical group: Intermediate/acid

Granulite is an even-textured high-grade metamorphic rock with weak or absent foliation. Often fine parallel bands of dark minerals run through the rock. Garnet-granulite and pyroxene-granulite are thought to be typical rocks from the lowermost continental crust. *Charnockite* is a variety with igneous interlocking texture, without garnet, but often containing hypersthene. Granulites occur in northwestern Scotland, Austria, Finland, Saxony in Germany, and India. Also as xenoliths in some continental volcanoes.

ID FACT FILE

TYPICAL MINERALS:
Alkali feldspar, plagioclase, quartz

OTHER MINERALS:
Pyroxene, garnet, cordierite, sillimanite, kyanite, scapolite

MINERAL PROPORTIONS:
Gneisslike but no mica; variable

GRAIN SIZE:
Medium- to fine-grained

COLOR:
Gray, brownish, greenish

TEXTURAL FEATURES:
Even-textured, sugary grain size; often finely banded

FOLIATION:
Weak; sometimes absent

CONDITIONS:
High pressure and high temperature

DISTRIBUTION:
Widespread, typical rock of lowermost crust

LOOKALIKES:
Hornfels does not occur over large regional distances

FAMILY: SCHIST

Greenschist

Chemical group: Basic/intermediate

The main minerals in greenschist contain iron, magnesium, and calcium, plus the feldspar albite. The greenish-colored mineral is usually chlorite, but many varieties of greenschist are dominated by different green minerals, such as *actinolite schist*, *chlorite schist*, and *talc schist*. Found in Argyle in Scotland, Hohe Tauern in Tyrol, Austria, Harz, Fichtelgebirge, and Bavaria in Germany, South Tyrol and Piedmonte in Italy, and in the Western Alps.

ID FACT FILE

TYPICAL MINERALS:
Chlorite, epidote, actinolite, albite

OTHER MINERALS:
Glaucophane, talc, calcite, magnetite, dolomite, quartz

MINERAL PROPORTIONS:
Abundant green minerals; quartz and orthoclase very minor or absent

GRAIN SIZE:
Fine-grained

COLOR:
Dark or light greenish gray

TEXTURAL FEATURES:
Even-textured rock, prominent platy weakness due to alignment of platy minerals (schist)

FOLIATION:
Distinct like schist

CONDITIONS:
Low–moderate pressure, moderate temperature

DISTRIBUTION:
Widespread; typical product of metamorphosed basic igneous rocks

LOOKALIKES:
Schist

Hornfels

Chemical group: Any

ID FACT FILE

TYPICAL MINERALS:
Andalusite,
biotite,
cordierite,
garnet,
hypersthene,
sillimanite,
quartz, feldspar

OTHER MINERALS:
Variable

MINERAL PROPORTIONS:
Variable;
substantial
feldspar

GRAIN SIZE:
Fine- to medium-
grained

COLOR:
Dark-colored,
gray, greenish,
black

TEXTURAL FEATURES:
Even-textured
rock, often
granular

FOLIATION:
None

CONDITIONS:
Low–moderate
pressure, high
temperature

DISTRIBUTION:
Contact
metamorphic
rock developed
adjacent to large
igneous
intrusions

LOOKALIKES:
Basalt,
amphibolite

Hornfels is the general name for hard rock developed in contact with large igneous intrusions. Hornfels often has a conchoidal fracture and is very tough and weather-resistant. Although it often contains many pale-colored minerals, the rock color is usually dark due to the very fine grain size. There are many varieties, the names of which are based on the dominant minerals, e.g. *andalusite hornfels* and *pyroxene hornfels*; other varieties are named after the precursor rock, as in *pelitic hornfels*. Found in Dartmoor, Cornwall, and Cumbria in England, Southern Uplands in Scotland, Vosges in France, Harz and Eifel in Germany, and southern Norway. Below: photomicrograph under crossed polars, greatly magnified.

FAMILY: PERIDOTITE

ID FACT FILE

TYPICAL MINERALS:
Olivine, diopside, enstatite

OTHER MINERALS:
Garnet, chromite, talc, serpentine

MINERAL PROPORTIONS:
>50% olivine (forsterite)

GRAIN SIZE:
Coarse-grained, granular; massive

COLOR:
Greenish, pale gray; reddish when altered

TEXTURAL FEATURES:
Even-textured, granular sometimes with banding

FOLIATION:
Absent to moderate

CONDITIONS:
High pressure and high temperature

DISTRIBUTION:
Locally common; restricted to uplifted core regions of mountain belts

LOOKALIKES:
Dunite

Lherzolite

Chemical group: Ultrabasic

Lherzolite is the most typical variety of olivine-rich rocks called peridotites; it contains mostly olivine, and smaller but similar amounts of enstatite and diopside. It is thought to be the dominant rock in the Earth's upper mantle. Its granular texture is developed under conditions of high pressure over long periods of time. Dark red garnet (pyrope) and small black grains of chromite are often present. During repeated metamorphism at lower pressure in the presence of water, the olivine in peridotite is replaced by serpentine and talc, sometimes producing serpentine rock (serpentinite; *see* p.212). Found in Lherz in the Pyrenees, the Central Alps, Cyprus, Ronda in Spain. Also as xenoliths in kimberlite and some volcanoes.

FAMILY: MARBLE

ID FACT FILE

TYPICAL MINERALS:
Calcite, dolomite

OTHER MINERALS:
Amphibole,
forsterite,
epidote, mica,
garnet,
magnetite,
plagioclase,
pyrite, quartz,
serpentine,
wollastonite

MINERAL PROPORTIONS:
Mostly carbonate

GRAIN SIZE:
Coarse-grained;
massive

COLOR:
White, pale
pinkish, greenish,
gray; variegated
or banded

TEXTURAL FEATURES:
Compact, often
wavy or stripy
appearance

FOLIATION:
None to well
foliated

CONDITIONS:
Low–moderate
pressure,
moderate–high
temperature

DISTRIBUTION:
Widespread in
mountain belts,
also around
igneous
intrusions

LOOKALIKES:
Limestone

Marble

Chemical group: Carbonate-rich

Marble is a coarsely crystalline calcite-rich metamorphic rock. It develops smooth, sometimes grooved, weathered surfaces and is sparkling or granular in broken surfaces. It is pale in color and translucent. Its even strength makes it a popular stone for building and ornamental purposes, although it is rather soft since it is made mostly of calcite. It is the typical product of metamorphosed limestone; a wide variety of minor minerals is often present. It can be distinguished from limestone by its lack of cavities, lack of fossils, and coarse-grain ("sparry") texture of shiny calcite grains. Found in Devon in England, Connemara in Ireland, Skye in Scotland, Tuscany and South Tyrol in Italy, Tyrol in Austria, France, Fichtelgebirge in Germany, Spain, and Greece.

Marble Variety

FAMILY: MIGMATITE

ID FACT FILE

Typical minerals:
Alkali feldspar, plagioclase, quartz, biotite

Other minerals:
Hornblende, garnet, cordierite, muscovite, sillimanite

Mineral proportions:
Alkali feldspar always present; quartz-rich segregations

Grain size:
Coarse; variable across outcrop

Color:
Often banded with white segregations

Textural features:
Prominent gneiss-like banding and interfingering of whitish segregations and snakelike folds

Foliation:
Weak to distinct, parallel to dark mica-rich bands

Conditions:
Low–high pressure, very high temperature

Distribution:
Widespread

Lookalikes:
Gneiss

Migmatite

Chemical group: Intermediate/acid

Migmatite appears as two intermingled rocks; usually the host gneiss is permeated white or light-colored granitelike rock. Migmatite represents one of the highest grades of regional metamorphism; the granite portion indicates a nearly-melted or partially melted condition (also called *anatexis*). Occurs in northwestern Scotland, the Central Alps, Brittany, and Auvergne in France, in Norway, Sweden, and Finland, and in the Black Forest and Bavaria in Germany, the Adirondacks, and Washington.

FAMILY: SCHIST

ID FACT FILE

TYPICAL MINERALS:
Mica, quartz

OTHER MINERALS:
Biotite, feldspar, chlorite, pyrophyllite, graphite, epidote

MINERAL PROPORTIONS:
Abundant mica (sericite)

GRAIN SIZE:
Fine-grained; speckled with occasional larger crystals

COLOR:
Pale silvery gray, pale greenish

TEXTURAL FEATURES:
Even-textured rock, flaky sericite wraps around other granular crystals; strong alignment and fine-scale wavy fabric

FOLIATION:
Prominent distinctive schist; cleaves into thin sheets

CONDITIONS:
Low–moderate pressure, moderate–high temperature

DISTRIBUTION:
Widespread

LOOKALIKES:
Other schists

Phyllite

Chemical group: Intermediate

Phyllite is a pale-colored schist rich in the mica sericite. It splits readily into thin sheets and has a distinctive silky luster on fresh surfaces. It contains a number of other flaky minerals whose parallel alignment produces sheetlike foliation. The presence of abundant quartz can be tested with hardness (scratches knife), but most other minerals are too small to identify even with a hand lens. Found in Cornwall in England, Vosges in France, Harz in Germany, Central Alps, Scandinavia, the northwest Highlands of Scotland. Below: enlargement with a hand lens.

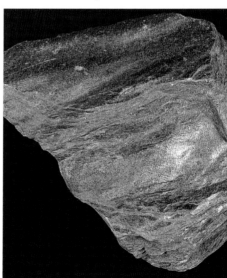

FAMILY: QUARTZITE

ID FACT FILE

TYPICAL MINERALS:
Quartz

OTHER MINERALS:
Any rock-forming minerals, e.g. feldspar, mica, chlorite, garnet

MINERAL PROPORTIONS:
Abundant quartz (>80%)

GRAIN SIZE:
Fine- to coarse-grained; massive

COLOR:
White, gray, brownish, reddish

TEXTURAL FEATURES:
Even-textured, massive

FOLIATION:
Absent or inconspicuous

CONDITIONS:
Low–moderate pressure, low–moderate temperature

DISTRIBUTION:
Widespread; typical product of metamorphosed sedimentary sandstone, quartz arenite

LOOKALIKES:
Sedimentary quartzite, sandstone

Quartzite
Chemical group: Acid

Quartzite forms thick weather-resistant layers in metamorphic mountain belts. Original sedimentary quartz grains are strongly cemented by further interlocking quartz, making a tough, often feature-forming rock. Small amounts of iron-rich minerals cause reddening. Some varieties contain enough mica to enable the rock to split into regular slabs. Irregular quartz grains are visible with a hand lens (*see* view below). Occurs in Anglesey in Wales, the Highlands in Scotland, Harz in Germany, Steiermark in Austria, in Scandinavia, and the Pyrenees in Spain.

Schist

Chemical group: Basic/intermediate

ID FACT FILE

TYPICAL MINERALS:
Essential platy minerals like mica, chlorite, amphibole, or talc

OTHER MINERALS:
Quartz, feldspar, epidote, graphite, garnet, cordierite, sillimanite, calcite, magnetite

MINERAL PROPORTIONS:
Variable

GRAIN SIZE:
Fine-grained, sometimes with coarser crystals

COLOR:
Often pale gray, greenish; distinctive sheen from reflective minerals

TEXTURAL FEATURES:
Parallel fabric of platy minerals; rock cleaves into platy pieces

FOLIATION:
Strong, often wavy

CONDITIONS:
Moderate–high pressure and temperature

DISTRIBUTION:
Widespread, large regions of old continental crust

LOOKALIKES:
Amphibolite, gneiss

Schist is a widely distributed metamorphic rock, recognized by its strong foliation and ease of parting. It is a textural rock name and wide mineral variations lead to many named varieties of schist. *Mica schist* with abundant muscovite, biotite, or chlorite is the usual recognizeable type, displaying shiny surfaces if broken. Dark red or brownish garnet in pale gray *garnet-mica schist* often weathers to rusty brown spots. Other varieties of schist are described separately. Occurs in Scotland, Connemara in Ireland, the Central Alps, Scandinavia, Germany, Central Pyrenees, France, and Spain.

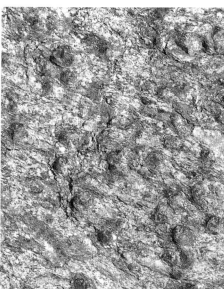

ID FACT FILE

TYPICAL MINERALS:
Serpentine

OTHER MINERALS:
Talc, calcite, olivine, pyroxene, amphibole, magnetite, garnet, chromite

MINERAL PROPORTIONS:
Abundant serpentine (chrysotile, antigorite)

GRAIN SIZE:
Fine- to coarse-grained

COLOR:
Dark green, greenish gray, dark red to black

TEXTURAL FEATURES:
Massive or fibrous; sometimes schistlike

FOLIATION:
Usually absent, but sometimes distinctive like schist

CONDITIONS:
Low–high pressure, low temperature

DISTRIBUTION:
Restricted product of metamorphosed ultramafic rocks

LOOKALIKES:
Peridotite

Serpentinite

Chemical group: Ultrabasic/basic

Serpentinite is a metamorphosed ultramafic rock where both olivine and pyroxene have been converted to serpentine minerals. Smaller amounts of a wide variety of minerals often include calcite and talc. A soft rock, it weathers to rounded shapes, is easily carved with a knife, and occurs in a wide variety of colors. Sometimes used for ornamental or decorative purposes, as in Lizard, Cornwall, in England. Found on Shetland Isles, in Scotland, in Austria, the Pyrenees, Switzerland, Liguria in Italy, Vosges in France, Fichtelgebirge in Germany, and in Troödos in Cyprus.

ID FACT FILE

TYPICAL MINERALS:
Calcite,
wollastonite,
diopside,
tremolite

OTHER MINERALS:
Dolomite, garnet,
vesuvianite,
serpentine,
quartz

MINERAL PROPORTIONS:
Variable, often
zoned

GRAIN SIZE:
Fine- to coarse-
grained

COLOR:
Pale gray,
greenish,
brownish

TEXTURAL FEATURES:
Granular,
sometimes
banded

FOLIATION:
None

CONDITIONS:
Low–moderate
pressure, high
temperature

DISTRIBUTION:
Restricted to
contact
metamorphosed
limestone around
igneous
intrusions

LOOKALIKES:
Marble

Skarn

Chemical group: Calcium-carbonate-silicate

Skarns are produced by contact
metamorphism of limestones. They change
progressively from rather pure carbonate
marble to bands made of various calcium-
magnesium silicate minerals, and finally to a
carbonate-free silicate rock. They are zoned
toward the igneous heat source. A common
pattern grades from unaltered dolomite to a
tremolite zone, then to a narrower diopside
zone and finally to an inner wollastonite and
garnet zone. Found in Skye in Scotland,
Dartmoor in England, Elba in Italy, Bavaria
in Germany, and in Sweden.

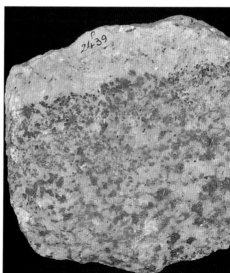

FAMILY: SLATE

ID FACT FILE

TYPICAL MINERALS:
Mica, chlorite,
quartz, feldspar

OTHER MINERALS:
Graphite, pyrite

MINERAL PROPORTIONS:
Abundant mica
and chlorite

GRAIN SIZE:
Very fine-grained

COLOR:
Dark gray,
greenish, bluish
gray

TEXTURAL FEATURES:
Even-textured
rock with
pronounced
uniform cleavage
direction

FOLIATION:
Distinctive slaty
cleavage, can be
split into thin
flakes

CONDITIONS:
Low pressure,
low temperature

DISTRIBUTION:
Widespread;
typical product of
metamorphosed
sedimentary
mudrocks

LOOKALIKES:
Unlikely to be
mistaken

Slate

Chemical group: Intermediate/acid

Slate results from low-grade regional
metamorphism of fine-grained sedimentary
mudrocks. The most obvious feature is the
presence of parallel planes of weakness, along
which the rock splits easily (cleavage), making
it distinct from original sedimentary bedding.
Fossils can be preserved, though they may be
deformed and partly replaced by pyrite. When
further heated during contact with a large
igneous intrusion, additional minerals, such as
andalusite, can give the slate a spotted
appearance. Widely used as a roofing material.
Found in Cumbria and Devon in England, in
Wales, Ardennes in France, and in
Fichtelgebirge and Saxony in Germany.

FAMILY: SILICICLASTIC SEDIMENT

Arkose

Chemical group: Acid

ID FACT FILE

TYPICAL COMPONENTS:
Quartz, feldspar, lithic fragments

OTHER COMPONENTS:
Hematite, calcite, clay, mica, resistant minerals

MATERIAL PROPORTIONS:
Feldspar>25%; much quartz and lithic fragments

GRAIN SIZE:
1/16 to 2 mm

COLOR:
Reddish brown, dark red

TEXTURAL FEATURES:
Continuous layering due to bedding planes; sedimentary structures and indications of mechanical sorting of grains

DISTRIBUTION:
Widespread surface-formed regional rock type known from all different geological ages

LOOKALIKES:
Sandstone

Arkose is a sedimentary rock with a high feldspar content (usually orthoclase or microcline), derived from weathering of feldspar-rich rocks like granites and gneisses. It contains some rock fragments and micas in a fine-grained matrix. The presence of hematite and iron staining cause the red coloration. Outcrop-scale features show evidence of sedimentation including, usually, bedding planes, sedimentary structures, and sorting of grains by layers. Occurs in Precambrian "Torridonian sandstone" in part and Devonian-aged rocks, "Old Red Sandstone" in part, as in Torridon in northwestern Scotland, Devon in England, and Vosges in France.

FAMILY: COARSE CLASTIC SEDIMENT

ID FACT FILE

TYPICAL COMPONENTS:
Lithic fragments, quartz and feldspar

OTHER COMPONENTS:
Hematite, calcite, clay, mica, resistant minerals

MATERIAL PROPORTIONS:
Variable

GRAIN SIZE:
Dominant mixture of granules (measuring a tiny fraction of an inch) to pebbles, locally with cobbles or even boulders up to 10 inches

COLOR:
Often brightly colored, yellow, reddish, gray

TEXTURAL FEATURES:
Unsorted mixture of grain sizes and angular clasts; originally porous then cemented by quartz, calcite, or clay minerals

DISTRIBUTION:
Restricted to continental areas with high relief, e.g. mountains

LOOKALIKES:
Conglomerate has rounded clasts and may be bedded

Breccia

Chemical group: Intermediate/acid

Breccia is a distinctive rock because of the presence of abundant angular and irregular-shaped rock fragments of varying sizes. The rock fragments vary widely depending on the source area. There is usually no sedimentary bedding and fossils are absent from the matrix. Slump breccias form by hillwash or landslide deposits; solution breccias result from cavity collapse and dissolution of evaporites beneath overlying rocks. Found in the Mendips in England, the Western Alps and Pyrenees in France and Spain, and South Tyrol and Sicily in Italy. *Tillite* is a hardened variety with boulders supported in a fine sand or clay matrix deposited under ice by ancient glaciations.

FAMILY: SILICEOUS SEDIMENT

ID FACT FILE

TYPICAL COMPONENTS:
Silica

OTHER COMPONENTS:
Minor clay, hematite

MATERIAL PROPORTIONS:
Mostly silica

GRAIN SIZE:
Very fine-grained, no visible crystals

COLOR:
Black, gray, greenish, or reddish

TEXTURAL FEATURES:
Very hard and compact, brittle fracture; occurs in bedded or nodular layers

DISTRIBUTION:
Moderate to deep water; bedded cherts may be associated with volcanic rocks. Widely distributed in rocks of all ages

LOOKALIKES:
Flint is a variety

Chert

Chemical group: Acid

Chert is composed almost entirely of very fine-grained silica, and includes some forms of opal and chalcedony. Its very fine grain size gives it a dark color. There are two types of chert. Bedded cherts can be extensive regional rock units, and may be related to hydrothermal activity or enhanced biochemical activity associated with volcanism. Nodular chert usually occurs in carbonate rocks as large irregular rounded lumps; small lumps in chalk are called *flint*. Biogenic silica, originally dispersed throughout the rock, for example as sponge spicules, is reprecipitated by fluids into the concentrations we see as chert. Found in Dover and Yorkshire in England, Ballantrae in Scotland, Montagne Noire in France, Mittelharz and Bavaria in Germany, the Pyrenees in Spain and France, and Cyprus.

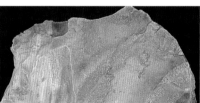

above chert   *below* flint

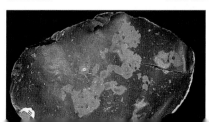

FAMILY: CLASTIC SEDIMENT

ID FACT FILE

TYPICAL COMPONENTS:
Clay minerals

OTHER COMPONENTS:
Quartz, feldspar, micas, calcite, rock dust

MATERIAL PROPORTIONS:
Rich in clay minerals

GRAIN SIZE:
Clay-sized muds (<$\frac{1}{256}$ mm) are finer than silts (<$\frac{1}{16}$ mm)

COLOR:
Gray, bluish, reddish, brownish, yellowish; variegated

TEXTURAL FEATURES:
Finely laminated, massive; deforms plastically when wet

DISTRIBUTION:
Old river systems, alluvial plains, lake basins

LOOKALIKES:
When dry resemble mudstones

Clay

Chemical group: Intermediate/acid

Clays and claystones contain abundant hydrous clay minerals, largely derived from weathering of feldspars in continental crustal rocks. Clay minerals require X-ray identification, and include kaolinite (*see* p.142), illite, and montmorillonite. Their variable colors are caused by additional minerals; limonite gives yellows, hematite browns and reds, sulfides gray, blue, and black. Water is trapped in clay, but clay itself is impermeable to water flow and is often used as a barrier. *Bentonite* is a gray-white variety often derived from weathering of volcanic ash. *Boulder clay* is a mixture of boulders in a rock flour and clay matrix formed by icy glaciers. Found in most countries, such as Jurassic-age Kimmeridge Clay in Yorkshire, England, and central and southern England.

FAMILY: ORGANIC/CARBONACEOUS SEDIMENT

ID FACT FILE

TYPICAL COMPONENTS:
Carbon, organic matter, fossils

OTHER COMPONENTS:
Minor clay, pyrite, quartz, calcite, dolomite, tar

MATERIAL PROPORTIONS:
Various organic compounds of carbon and hydrocarbons

GRAIN SIZE:
Very fine-grained, no visible crystals

COLOR:
Black, brown

TEXTURAL FEATURES:
Occurs in bedded or slightly nodular layers often with shales and sandstones in repetitive sequences

DISTRIBUTION:
Shallow water, estuaries, swamps; older higher grade coals occur in folded mountain belts

LOOKALIKES:
Unlikely to be mistaken (black streak)

Coal

Chemical group: Organic

Coals are formed from the accumulation and maturation of plant materials. *Peat*, as currently found in moors and fens, is related to coals but is uncompacted and immature. *Anthracite* is the most carbon-rich mature form of coal, the highest grade with more than 90 percent carbon. It is a bright shiny rock with conchoidal fracture. During maturation of coals, large quantities of hydrocarbon gases, like methane, are released. High-grade coals are generally older, such as those that developed in the Carboniferous age of western Europe. Found in Durham, in Northumberland and Yorkshire in England, in South Wales, the Midland Valley, in Scotland, and Essen and Ruhr in Germany.

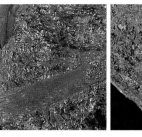

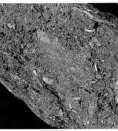

above left coal
above peat
left anthracite coal

ID FACT FILE

TYPICAL COMPONENTS:
Lithic fragments, quartz, feldspar

OTHER COMPONENTS:
Hematite, calcite, clay, mica, resistant minerals

MATERIAL PROPORTIONS:
Variable

GRAIN SIZE:
Dominant mixture of granules (measuring a tiny fraction of an inch) to pebbles, locally with cobbles or even boulders up to 10 inches

COLOR:
Often brightly colored, yellow, reddish, gray

TEXTURAL FEATURES:
Poorly sorted mixture of grain sizes and rounded clasts; cemented by quartz, calcite, or clay minerals. May show some bedding or poor grading

DISTRIBUTION:
Sedimentary basins

LOOKALIKES:
Breccia has angular clasts and is unsorted

Conglomerate

Chemical group: Acid

Conglomerate is a coarse clastic rock with distinctive rounded pebbles and other sized clasts of older rocks. Polymict conglomerates show a wide variety of rock types, whereas monomict conglomerates consist of one rock type only e.g. limestone conglomerate. Conglomerates accumulate within sedimentary basins and alluvial fans or old gravel deposits; they may be clast-supported or matrix-supported. Found in Devon in England, Torridon in Scotland, Upper Bavaria in Germany, Wallis in Switzerland, Sicily in Italy, the Pyrenees in France and Spain. Hertfordshire *Puddingstone* (shown) is a colorful quartz-cemented variety of Eocene age (45 million years) from central England.

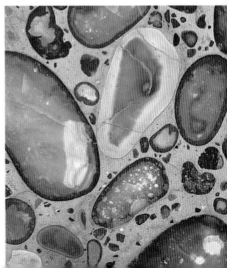

FAMILY: CARBONATE SEDIMENT

ID FACT FILE

TYPICAL
COMPONENTS:
Dolomite, calcite

OTHER COMPONENTS:
Fossil debris,
clay, quartz

MATERIAL
PROPORTIONS:
>50% dolomite

GRAIN SIZE:
Usually fine- to
medium-grained

COLOR:
Shades of brown,
gray, yellowish,
or reddish

TEXTURAL FEATURES:
Usually even-
textured, often
poorly bedded,
may be porous

DISTRIBUTION:
As for
limestones

LOOKALIKES:
Limestone reacts
more vigorously
with acid

Dolomite

Chemical group: Carbonate

Dolomite shares the same name as the mineral
(dolomite, *see* p.67) of which it is largely
composed. In all other respects, it shares the
same features as limestone. It reacts more
slowly with acid than calcite-rich limestone,
and is also often notably more dense. It may
form during the passage of water through
ordinary limestone, when extra magnesium
(needed for the mineral dolomite) is fixed in
the rock. All intermediate proportions of
dolomite and calcite varieties of limestone are
known. Dolomite may occur interbedded with
limestone, and is more resistant to weathering.
Found in northern England, Jura in France,
South Tyrol in Italy and the mountains of the
same name, and the Dolomites in Italy.

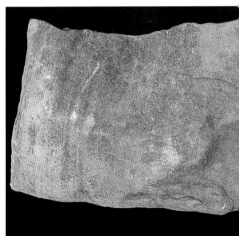

FAMILY: CHEMICAL SEDIMENT

Evaporite

Chemical group: Saline

Evaporites form by precipitation of minerals directly from water, during evaporation of trapped saline fluids, in trapped lagoons, salt lakes, or intertidal zones, as in the Dead Sea between Israel and Jordan, and Great Salt Lake, Utah. Precipitation is often cyclic and gives a banded or laminated appearance. Evaporite rocks are easily disturbed, and may be partly dissolved, leading to collapse and formation of angular pieces (breccia). Rocks of just one mineral type are common. Rock salt is made almost entirely of halite, and gypsum rock is a variety of massive gypsum often with nodular or coarsely crystalline forms of twinned or fibrous gypsum. Substantial old evaporite deposits may represent lost seas. Found in Cheshire in England (Permian), Zechstein in Germany (Permian), Moscow Basin (Devonian), and the Dead Sea (Miocene).

FAMILY: SILICICLASTIC SEDIMENT

ID FACT FILE

TYPICAL COMPONENTS:
Quartz, feldspar, lithic fragments

OTHER COMPONENTS:
Hematite, mica, resistant minerals

MATERIAL PROPORTIONS:
Abundant quartz, feldspar, and lithic fragments

GRAIN SIZE:
From very fine up to ⅖ inch

COLOR:
Dark gray, greenish gray, or black

TEXTURAL FEATURES:
Obvious quartz plus other mineral grains and rock fragments in a very fine-grained matrix (silt-sized); often bedded and graded

DISTRIBUTION:
Regional rock type associated with active geological periods of mountain building and volcanism

LOOKALIKES:
Dolerite

Graywacke

Chemical group: Intermediate/acid

Graywacke has a characteristic very fine-grained matrix (silt-sized or mud) surrounding prominent sand-sized grains of quartz, lithic fragments, and feldspar (mostly plagioclase). They can show sedimentary structures indicative of rapid accumulation and vigorous water currents. Indicators of enhanced tectonic or volcanic activity, they are often formed in basins. Found in Wales, in Ireland, Southern Uplands in Scotland, Devon in England, Westphalia in Germany. They also form many of the Cretaceous-Tertiary erosional deposits in the Alps.

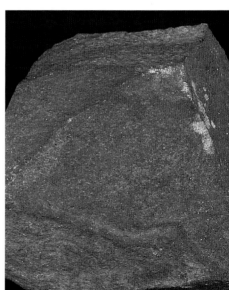

FAMILY: IRON-RICH SEDIMENT

Ironstone

Chemical group: Intermediate/acid

ID FACT FILE

TYPICAL COMPONENTS:
Quartz, feldspar, hematite, siderite

OTHER COMPONENTS:
Magnetite, goethite, glauconite, pyrite, and other iron minerals, clay, calcite

MATERIAL PROPORTIONS:
>15% iron oxides by weight

GRAIN SIZE:
Variable clastic and chemical sediments

COLOR:
Dark brown, reddish, yellowish

TEXTURAL FEATURES:
Banded laminated or oolitic with sedimentary structures; also nodular or massive

DISTRIBUTION:
Ancient (Precambrian) ironstones formed in deep water basins; younger ones in shallow to deep water

LOOKALIKES:
Distinguished by higher density (SG)

Ancient ironstones often consist of banded hematite and magnetite layers interbedded with cherts and sandstones. They are an important economic source of iron. Younger oolitic ironstones often consist of rounded pellets called ooids cemented by hematite, goethite, or siderite. Recent ironstones are represented by iron and manganese-rich nodules on the deep ocean floor. Ancient banded ironstones occur outside of Europe, as around Lake Superior in Ontario, Canada, northwestern Australia, and South Africa. Oolitic ironstones are found in Palaeozoic carbonate sediments as in South Wales, Northampton, and Westbury in England, Lorraine in France, and Luxembourg. *Ocher* is a brightly colored red/yellow goethite/limonite-rich massive variety; *umber* is a finely laminated dark brown siltstone (*see* opposite). Umber and ocher occur with hydrothermal volcanic deposits from active seafloor spreading ridges as in the Cretaceous deposits of Cyprus.

Ironstone Varieties

Chemical group: Intermediate/acid

red ocher

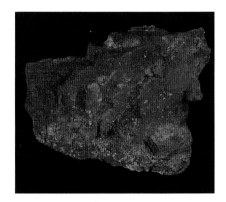

yellow ocher

umber

FAMILY: CARBONATE SEDIMENT

ID FACT FILE

TYPICAL COMPONENTS:
Calcite, fossil debris

OTHER COMPONENTS:
Dolomite, siderite, quartz, feldspar, mica, clay

MATERIAL PROPORTIONS:
Abundant calcite, up to ~95%

GRAIN SIZE:
From very fine mud to coarse gravel

COLOR:
White, gray, yellowish, reddish, greenish, or black

TEXTURAL FEATURES:
Usually bedded, often crowded with fossils

DISTRIBUTION:
Continental shelves, shallow seas, oceanic islands, lakes

LOOKALIKES:
Unlikely to be mistaken (except for dolomite); carbonate minerals react with acid

Limestone

Chemical group: Carbonate

Limestones are formed as biochemical or biological precipitates of carbonate minerals, and are very variable. They can form as carbonate muds, or from the accumulated carbonate-rich skeletons of fossils, as reefs, or in tidal flats. They may be porous, fine-grained, or coarse-grained. The principle sources of the carbonates are the skeletons of many organisms including algae, corals, sponges, shelly fossils, crustacea, and others. They can be subdivided on the basis of their grain shapes, or cements, or grain size. *Oolitic limestone* (*see* below) is a variety formed of rounded concretions that are less than $\frac{2}{25}$ inch in size (ooids) and resemble fish eggs; it develops in shallow water. *Chalk* (*see* opposite) is a famous fine-grained white-colored and often porous variety made from hard parts of algae and microfossils; it is sometimes associated with nodules of chert or flint. Reef limestone is an unbedded variety formed through continuous deposition of calcareous reef organisms like corals, algae, bryozoa, shelly fossils, and sponges.

FAMILY: CARBONATE SEDIMENT

Limestone Variety: Chalk

Chemical group: Carbonate

FAMILY: SILICEOUS SEDIMENT

ID FACT FILE

TYPICAL COMPONENTS:
Silica, microfossils

OTHER COMPONENTS:
Minor clay, hematite

MATERIAL PROPORTIONS:
Mostly silica

GRAIN SIZE:
Fine- to medium-grained

COLOR:
Gray, greenish, or brownish

TEXTURAL FEATURES:
Dense rock, breaks with a brittle edge; abundant visible microfossils (may require hand lens)

DISTRIBUTION:
Exclusively seawater-derived; old rocks in mountain belts

LOOKALIKES:
Chert

Radiolarite

Chemical group: Acid

Radiolarite is a siliceous rock made of the skeletons of myriad siliceous microfossils called radiolaria. Soft siliceous muds or oozes are accumulating on the deep ocean floors today; radiolaria are common in equatorial regions. Occasional radiolarites contain microfossils that measure up to ⅟₁₆ inch but the microfossils are usually much smaller and only clearly visible with a hand lens. Found in Bohemia in the Czech Republic, Hohe Tauern in Austria, Corsica in France, and in Bavaria in Germany.

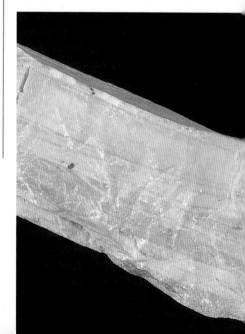

FAMILY: CLASTIC SEDIMENT

Sandstone

Chemical group: Acid

ID FACT FILE

TYPICAL COMPONENTS:
Quartz

OTHER COMPONENTS:
Calcite, feldspar, clay, mica, resistant minerals

MATERIAL PROPORTIONS:
Quartz dominant

GRAIN SIZE:
$\frac{1}{16}$ to 2 mm

COLOR:
Whitish, gray, yellowish, red, brown

TEXTURAL FEATURES:
Prominent continuous layering due to bedding planes; sedimentary structures and indications of mechanical sorting of grains

DISTRIBUTION:
Widespread surface-formed regional rock type known from all different geological ages

LOOKALIKES:
Grades into siltstone (finer-grained) and conglomerates (coarser-grained)

Sandstone contains particles large enough to see with the naked eye and is always layered (bedding planes). It represents consolidated and cemented mechanical deposits of sands. Sands transported longer distances become richer in quartz, due to its hardness and resistance to weathering. Sandstone is often somewhat porous. Mechanical sorting (as for other clastic sediments) produces sandstone with a small range of grain sizes. Angular grains imply a short transportation distance. Sandstones represent old fluvial, deltaic, and channel deposits and are frequently fossiliferous. Sandstone also occurs widely as wind-transported desert sands, which often show cross bedding. A very popular building stone, it occurs in South Wales, the Midlands and north of England, the Midland Valley in Scotland, and in the Rhine Valley in Germany.

FAMILY: CLASTIC SEDIMENT

Sandstone Variety: Glauconitic Sandstone

Chemical group: Acid

ID FACT FILE

TYPICAL COMPONENTS:
Quartz

OTHER COMPONENTS:
Calcite, feldspar, clay, mica, resistant minerals

MATERIAL PROPORTIONS:
Quartz dominant; presence of glauconite

GRAIN SIZE:
⅟₁₆ to 2 mm

COLOR:
Whitish, gray, yellowish, red, brown

TEXTURAL FEATURES:
Prominent continuous layering due to bedding planes; sedimentary structures and indications of mechanical sorting of grains

DISTRIBUTION:
Widespread surface-formed regional rock type known from all different geological ages

LOOKALIKES:
Grades into siltstone (finer-grained) and conglomerates (coarser-grained)

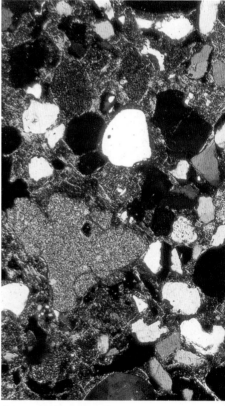

Petrographic thin section, view much enlarged (×25) shows rounded to angular quartz (white and gray) and irregular grains of glauconite (red and brown).

FAMILY: CLASTIC SEDIMENT

ID FACT FILE

TYPICAL COMPONENTS:
Clay, fine-grained silt

OTHER COMPONENTS:
Clay, quartz, mica, carbonate, organic compounds

MATERIAL PROPORTIONS:
>50% clay or rock powder (silt); may contain fossils

GRAIN SIZE:
Less than $\frac{1}{16}$ mm

COLOR:
Gray, brownish, greenish, reddish

TEXTURAL FEATURES:
Prominent partings, and fine laminations due to bedding planes; uniform appearance, sometimes with small rounded harder concretions or nodules

DISTRIBUTION:
Widespread; one of the commonest sedimentary rocks

LOOKALIKES:
Slate is much harder with cleavage

Shale

Chemical group: Intermediate/acid

Mudstones are the commonest sedimentary rocks. Shale is a consolidated variety of clay-rich mudstone with a well developed parting, enabling it to split easily into thin sheets. For this property it is said to be "fissile." Mudstones are deposited in river floodplains, lakes, deltas, continental slopes, and seafloors. Like mudstones in general, shale is easily weathered and produces subdued topography. Some shales include rounded nodules of carbonate minerals, pyrite, or chert. Shale frequently occurs interbedded with coarser-grained sedimentary rocks, sometimes as regular repetitions forming sandstone-shale sequences. *Oil shale* is a dark gray or black variety rich in organic materials. *Marl* is a variety of mudstone that is rich in carbonates, formed as carbonate mud (*see* p.232). Found in England, Wales, Scotland, France, Germany and most European countries.

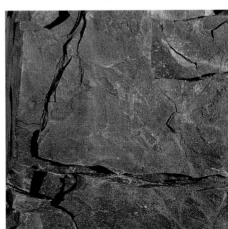

Shale Varieties

Chemical group: Intermediate/acid

ID FACT FILE

TYPICAL COMPONENTS:
Clay, fine-grained silt

OTHER COMPONENTS:
Clay, quartz, mica, carbonate, organic compounds

MATERIAL PROPORTIONS:
>50% clay or rock powder (silt); may contain fossils

GRAIN SIZE:
Less than 1/16 mm

COLOR:
Gray, brownish, greenish, reddish

TEXTURAL FEATURES:
Prominent partings and fine laminations due to bedding planes; uniform appearance, sometimes with small rounded harder concretions or nodules

DISTRIBUTION:
Widespread; one of the commonest sedimentary rocks

LOOKALIKES:
Slate is much harder with cleavage

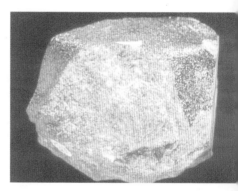

Marl

Oil shale

FAMILY: CARBONATE SEDIMENT

ID FACT FILE

Typical components:
Calcite, dolomite

Other components:
Aragonite, minor clay

Material proportions:
Mostly calcite

Grain size:
Very fine-grained, no visible crystals

Color:
Whitish, pale gray, pinkish, yellowish

Textural features:
Porous, irregular fine-scale banding

Distribution:
Formed around hot springs

Lookalikes:
Marble, limestone

Travertine

Chemical group: Carbonate

Travertine is a porous variety of terrestrial limestone, formed as a chemical precipitate from waters emanating from hot springs. The fine laminations and banding reflect different growth layers. Can be almost pure calcite and, but for its high porosity, superficially resembles marble. Can also contain dolomite and aragonite, but these can be difficult to identify due to the very fine grain size. Found in the Sabine Mountains in Central Italy, and in Württemburg and Thuringia in Germany.

FAMILY: IMPACTITE

ID FACT FILE

TYPICAL
COMPONENTS:
Glass and
various silicate
minerals

OTHER COMPONENTS:
Rock fragments

MATERIAL
PROPORTIONS:
Variable

COLOR:
Dark-colored,
greenish, black

TEXTURAL FEATURES:
Massive rock,
usually mostly
glass, no gas
voids and very
compact;
sometimes finely
crystalline with
small clusters of
silicate minerals,
or feathery
quench crystals

DISTRIBUTION:
Rare rock but
occurs within
large impact
craters (>approx
37 miles)

LOOKALIKES:
Similar to
volcanic glass
but massive;
sometimes
contains spinifex
textures (see
komatiite;
p.167)

Impactite

Chemical group: Silica-rich

Impactite is an extreme variety of metamorphic rock that forms by shock metamorphism (melting or anatexis) resulting from a large crater-forming impact. Pressures and temperatures are so high that the target rocks melt within seconds; some unmelted relics of crustal silicate rocks survive. Impactite can contain tiny diamonds formed by the shock pressure; sometimes feathery silicate textures (spinifex) occur. Impactite can form large bodies of glassy rock up to several miles in size; *tagamite* is the local name for impactite at the large 60-mile-diameter Popigai crater in Siberia. As for true volcanic glass, impactite glass weathers easily to clay minerals. Also found at the Ries crater, Germany, Chicxulub crater, Mexico, and Charlevoix crater, Canada.

14-million-year-old
impactite from
Ries crater

Iron Meteorite

Chemical group: Iron-rich

ID FACT FILE

TYPICAL COMPONENTS:
Iron with nickel

OTHER COMPONENTS:
Graphite, troilite (FeS)

MATERIAL PROPORTIONS:
Mostly solid iron

COLOR:
Metallic iron, dark distinctive crust; weathers brown

TEXTURAL FEATURES:
Fresh interior of metallic iron, when polished shows coarse elongated criss-crossing grains; may have small rounded inclusions of soft black graphite. The exterior is usually rusty brown with altered iron oxides/hydroxides and may be pitted and scalloped

TESTS:
Notable high density of nickel-iron (SG 6–7)

DISTRIBUTION:
A common class of meteorite, due to its resistance to weathering and ability to penetrate the Earth's atmosphere

LOOKALIKES:
Unlikely to be mistaken

All meteorites are rare; of these, iron meteorites are relatively common. They are coarsely crystalline alloys of iron and nickel (typically 7–15 percent nickel), with small admixtures of additional trace metals, including gold and iridium. The crystalline textures revealed on prepared smooth surfaces etched with acid are known as *Widmanstatten* structure; it can only be produced by very slow cooling, perhaps in parent asteroids a few hundred miles in size. Iron meteorites were all formed within a short period of time of the birth of the Solar System around 4,550 million years ago. *Hexahedrite* is a variety with low nickel (~7%), *octahedrite* has high nickel (~40%), and *ataxite* is nickel-rich but lacks the Widmanstatten structure perhaps as a result of reheating.

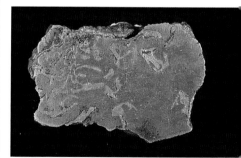

Martian Meteorite

Chemical group: Silicate-rich; basic/ultrabasic

Martian meteorites are made of the same silicate minerals that occur on Earth, and resemble basic igneous rocks, although some also contain unusual black glass formed by shock melting. Unlike most other meteorites, which have ages of 4,550 millon years, these are very young with ages to 180 million years. One famous Martian meteorite contains small microscopic shapes in carbonate minerals, which resemble microfossils; this meteorite (ALH84001, illustrated) provided in 1996 the first evidence for a "fossilized Martian biota." As with most meteorites, Martian meteorites often have a distinctive black *fusion crust*.

Stony Meteorite

Chemical group: Silicate-rich

ID FACT FILE

ESSENTIAL MINERALS:
Pyroxene, olivine,
or plagioclase

OTHER MINERALS:
Nickel-rich iron,
graphite, spinel,
chromite

COLOR:
Dark gray,
greenish, black;
mottled

TEXTURAL FEATURES:
Fine-grained
silicate minerals,
often with small
pea-sized
rounded
inclusions
(chondrules).
Matrix can be
very fine-grained,
sometimes with
fragments of
glass or metallic
iron

TESTS:
Dark crusty
surface texture
can be
distinctive

DISTRIBUTION:
The most
abundant class
of meteorite

LOOKALIKES:
Similar to fine-
grained gabbro,
peridotite, picrite

All meteorites are rare; stony meteorites are the most common family. Most meteorites have a dark "rind" or fusion crust caused by heating during flight through the atmosphere. They are made of the same silicate minerals (bronzite, diopside, olivine, and plagioclase) that occur in terrestrial gabbro, plus occasional glass and small amounts of nickel-rich iron. Most of them contain rounded *chondrules* in a fine-grained matrix, sometimes with fragments of glass or metallic nickel-iron and are called *chondrites*; those without are much less common and are called *achondrites*. They contain small amounts of microscopic diamonds.

FAMILY: STONY-IRON METEORITE

Stony-iron Meteorite

Chemical group: Silicate and iron metal

ID FACT FILE

TYPICAL COMPONENTS:
Pyroxene, olivine, or plagioclase plus substantial nickel iron metal

OTHER COMPONENTS:
Occasional tridymite

MATERIAL PROPORTIONS:
Iron metal silicates

COLOR:
Dark gray, greenish, black; mottled, gemmy

TEXTURAL FEATURES:
Large silicate crystals in a matrix of nickel-iron metal; or the reverse relationship

TESTS:
Dark crusty surface texture can be distinctive

DISTRIBUTION:
The rarest family of meteorites

LOOKALIKES:
Although transitional between iron and stony meteorites, this family has highly distinctive textures, very different to terrestrial rocks

Meteorites are rare but stony-iron meteorites are rarest, forming less than 10 percent of all meteorites. They are mixtures of silicate minerals (bronzite, diopside, olivine, and plagioclase) and substantial amounts of nickel-rich iron. *Mesosiderite* contains chunks of nickel-iron metal, angular fragments of silicate rock (bronzite, olivine, and plagioclase), glass, and metal veins. *Pallasite* contains large, often gem-quality olivines (peridote) up to half an inch in size in a connected metal matrix; these are thought to have come from the cores of large asteroids like Vesta (310 miles in size). The photograph shows pallasite; the pale hollows are eroded olivines.

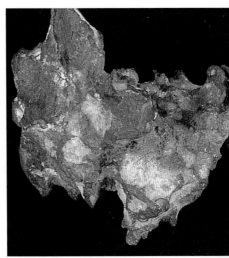

FAMILY: IMPACTITE

ID FACT FILE

TYPICAL COMPONENTS:
Silicate rock fragments and impact glass (may be altered)

OTHER COMPONENTS:
Any

COLOR:
Gray, speckled, greenish, brownish, dark

TEXTURAL FEATURES:
Angular fragments of all sizes of rocks and minerals, including dark fragments of partly porous glass, in a fine-grained matrix. Usually silicate-rich or carbonate-rich. Sometimes layered or bedded; occasional levels of impact lapilli (*see* tuff; p.175)

TESTS:
Association with impact crater features

DISTRIBUTION:
Rare rock but occurs within large impact craters (>approx 12 miles)

LOOKALIKES:
Breccia, ignimbrite, tuff

Suevite

Chemical group: Silica-rich or carbonate-rich

Suevites are mixed rocks containing some dispersed impact melt. They are composed of fragments of partly porous impact glass, glass bombs, numerous fragments of crystalline, and sedimentary rocks in a matrix of the same materials but finer-grained. Some rock fragments are highly shocked, others are barely affected; even fossils may be preserved. They may contain microscopic diamonds and other minerals indicative of very high shock pressure, such as coesite and stishovite (*see* quartz; p.124). Found at the Ries crater in Germany, Popigai crater in Siberia, Chicxulub crater in Mexico, and the Haughton crater, Canada. The photograph is of suevite from the Ries crater.

FAMILY: TEKTITE

ID FACT FILE

TYPICAL COMPONENTS:
Glass

OTHER COMPONENTS:
Usually none

COLOR:
Black, yellowish, brown, green

TEXTURAL FEATURES:
Smooth rounded shapes, sometimes flattened, with distinctive pitted, grooved, or fluted surfaces

TESTS:
Conchoidal fracture. Translucent to transparent in thin flakes

DISTRIBUTION:
Very widespread as clasts in both continental and oceanic sediments; restricted in age to youngish rocks (Tertiary–Recent)

LOOKALIKES:
Volcanic glass, obsidian

Tektite

Chemical group: Acid

Tektites occur as vast sprayed fields of liquid melted rock that has been jetted from large meteorite impacts within continental crust. Their shapes form as tear-shaped drops with viscous draglines on the surface (the grooves and flutes). They are very rich in silica; thin flakes are translucent to transparent and show their true colors. They are named after the regions in which they occur, such as *thailandite* (Thailand), *australasite* (Australia), and georgite (Georgia). *Moldavite* is a bottle-green variety from Moldavia in the Czech Republic related to the 15-mile diameter Ries impact crater in southern Germany (age 15 million years) that lies some 250 miles away.

INDEX

Main entries are given in **bold**.